GARDEN PEONIES

by

James Kelway

Second edition, revised and updated

by

Dave Root

Picts Hill Publishing

2013

Kelways Heritage Series No. 2

First published   1954
Second edition   2013

Copyright © Dave Root

The moral right of the author has been asserted in accordance with the
Copyright, Designs and Patents Act 1988.

Published in hardback in the United Kingdom in 2013 by
Picts Hill Publishing an imprint of Even Handed Licensing Limited

ISBN **978-1-904496-08-3**

Printed in Great Britain by the Somerton Printery

Picts Hill Publishing
Even Handed Licensing Limited
PO Box 93
Langport
TA10 1AP

Cover picture   *P. Tamafuyo*

Kelways Heritage Series
1. Janet Seaton. *Kelway's Glorious: the story of a pioneering Somerset nursery*.
(Picts Hill Publishing, 2011)
2. James Kelway and Dave Root. *Garden Peonies.*
(Picts Hill Publishing, 2013)

The Peony Valley

PREFACE TO THE FIRST EDITION

It seems to me surprising as well as unfortunate that the peony, one of the loveliest of all flowers and available to all who own a plot of ground, is not as widely known to the general public in Britain as it is in the United States of America. If, in the following pages, I can in some small measure, remedy this I shall indeed be glad, for I have spent a long life cultivating and popularising these beautiful flowers, which have rewarded me with the purest pleasure. I have written this book to make the charm and the variety of the peony more widely known, and all the information given refers entirely to varieties suitable for general cultivation. Those who may be interested in a botanical account of the genus Paeonia and of its series of exotic species may be directed to F.C.Stern's *A Study of the Genus Paeonia*, a monumental work of unique research, published by the Royal Horticultural Society. This little book is a labour of love, addressed to garden lovers.

James Kelway
1952

First Edition 1954

PREFACE TO THE SECOND EDITION

James Kelway, the author of the first edition of this book, died on August 8th 1952, at the age of 81. The original book was published in 1954, two years after his death. It is a charming and enjoyable read for anyone that loves peonies (the more usual modern spelling). As the current head of Kelways, it is my privilege to bring this book back into print after nearly 60 years. The text is largely as written by James Kelway. An updated section on pest and disease prevention and control has been included. I have amended plant names in line with current nomenclature. Some of the varieties listed in the original book are not readily available any more, or have long since been lost to cultivation. These have been omitted, and other varieties added that were also familiar to and grown by James Kelway. These have been described where possible using his own words from Kelways nursery records. Other, more recent introductions have been added to bring this book up to date with some of the incredible advances in breeding and superb new cultivars that have been introduced in the last 60 years, which have substantially increased the colour range and flowering period of the peony. The chapter on tree peonies has been rewritten to include in particular, the latest Intersectional hybrids: crosses between herbaceous and tree peonies, which were unimaginable at the time this book was originally written.

Dave Root
2013

Contents

INTRODUCTION

The peony is one of those plants, which after years of neglect, has become popular again among gardeners. Some the earliest varieties bred over 150 years ago are still garden worthy. Yet exquisite new varieties have been developed with all the hardy qualities of the common cottage garden peony, but with colours rivalling even the roses. No man did more to establish the peony in its rightful place than the late James Kelway (1871-1952), whose tremendous enthusiasm and unique experience is reflected in these pages.

The herbaceous peony is one of the easiest plants to cultivate, wanting little more than room. It flowers in May and June before the roses, thus providing a focus of interest in the garden in that possible blank patch between spring and summer profusion. It is a wonderful plant for cutting; its extraordinarily decorative foliage, changing colour as the season advances, would be worth cultivating even if the plant did not flower, while the spectacular effect of its blooms; pink, white and cream as well as crimson, is unrivalled.

Peonies have often had a bad press, claiming that they are fickle characters, with the personality of a diva, with a too short flowering period. It is true, that each plant has its moment...*but what a moment it is!* By choosing a selection of types even a small garden can have peonies in bloom from late April right up to the last week of June, and sometimes even into July. Within the pages of this small handbook is everything the gardener needs to know about how to get the best from these most wonderful and gracious of garden plants.

CHAPTER I

The characteristics of the peony

Of the hardy perennial herbaceous plants, which flower in early summer, the members of the peony family are, in my view, the most beautiful and desirable. Although I have been closely associated from childhood with other leading flower families: gladioli, delphiniums, pyrethrums and lupins amongst them, the peony has my undoubted preference over them all.

The habit of the plant, the form and colouring of its foliage, the infinite variety, beauty, profusion and fragrance of its flowers, as well as its extreme hardiness, vigour and ease of culture, make the peony, in my estimation, the best of all the hardy perennial non-shrubby plants for gardens in these islands, and indeed in any country of the temperate and sub-arctic zones. The very carriage of the plant raises it above other hardy plants of its season, and indeed no border plant which succeeds it during the year, has a more distinguished appearance. The modern delphinium is superb in foliage and flower colour but has no scent and the blooms lack the variety of form and colour tones, which the peony displays. Nor does the plant flower so early in the year. The rose and rhododendron, being shrubs, are outside the comparison.

The sheer loveliness of the blooms of the June-flowering varieties, and of the "tree" or shrubby kinds, is so extraordinary that it seems impossible to find words for the innumerable colour values, the texture of petal and the purity and symmetry of line and outline of many of the large, handsome blossoms. "Colour charts", while helpful, are not completely satisfactory; for gradations of tints perceptible by the sensitive eye must be gathered under one colour-name in any published chart. For colour is not only dependent upon the kind of light reflected from the surface of the object, but also by the texture of the surface. The flowers of the peony are particularly affected by alterations in the light. The flowers, magnificent in full sunlight at noon, are still more stimulating early in the morning or towards sunset when the horizontal rays of the sun penetrate the petals and make them glow with life, while they tip with fire such flowers as are above the half shadows. Peonies in large numbers, seen thus, are never to be forgotten. When I took the late William Robinson, author of *The English Flower Garden*, into the midst of scores of thousands of peony plants in a valley, he exclaimed that he could recall no lovelier sight from his wide experience of gardens and floral landscapes the world over.

P. Festiva Maxima (p45)

Peonies are bold as well as gracious beauties, prodigal of their loveliness, giving you all they have; you have not to search for it, and there are no thorns. One large plant may produce from forty to fifty magnificent flowers borne on stiff erect stems above a bush of foliage, which is highly decorative in itself. The height of the plants, from about two and a half to four feet (75-120cm), is ideal for appreciation; there is no need to stoop to admire; they are just under your nose, the exact and proper place, for flowers, which are so sweetly scented.

The delicate suavity of the perfume of most of the *P. lactiflora* types, so different from that of the well-known old double crimson (*P. officinalis*), would alone place them in the first rank of garden flowers. Some smell of roses (whence came, as well as from their shape, the old name "piny-roses"), others of honey and fragrant spices. The scent arising in the evening of a hot day from a large planting could persuade you that you were standing near a mammoth potpourri bowl. In the house, their fragrance is especially agreeable; for unlike that of some flowers in a confined space, it does not become overpowering or unpleasant.

As I have already said, in addition to their colour and fragrance, peonies have a further attraction in their great variability. This is displayed not merely in the colour but also in the form of their flowers, in the arrangement of the petals and of the curious, jewel-like petaloids in the centre of some of the singles and semi-doubles; in the outline both of each petal and of the whole flower, and in the protean changes from the bud stage through maturity to age. This variation in form and colour is a matter of great interest and excitement to the connoisseur; peonies are the least predictable of plants. I do not mean that a red peony can change to a white, or a pink to a purple, or a single to a double, but the description of the form and colour of a flower cannot always be exact.

A great many of the varieties vary surprisingly, for example, with the strength of the plants. Some varieties which are two-coloured or many coloured, with central petals of a different tint from the outside collars when produced by plants which are not at the height of their strength, become on strong plants fully double and nearly of one colour; the smaller petals make way for larger petals of the same shade as the outside ones. It is usual in describing a variety to take the colour when the flower first opens, but many varieties of delicate shades gradually become white as they are exposed to strong sunlight, and regain the beauty of their particular tone of colour when in shadow.

P. Shirley Temple (p51)

The more one knows peonies the more they fascinate, and with increasing eagerness one looks forward to the time when they will be in flower again early the next summer. A devotee will find pleasure in recording notes of their individual characteristics. And so for some of us the most exciting moment each year is when the first peony bud opens towards the end of

May or early in June. One has watched the plants for many weeks, from the day in February or March when the "dear rosy snouts", as Miss Jekyll called them, poked silently above the ground and slowly closed their ranks Some quicker and therefore taller than others, some in green, others in red coats. It is difficult to name any plant, which makes its first appearance above ground with such a startling depth of colour. One of my favourite colours in the paint-box when I was a boy was called "Crimson lake" and this to me best describes the hue of most of these spear-like stems. As the spears become crowned with banners of foliage many other colour descriptions have to be used, such as ruby red, chrysanthemum crimson, purple madder, garnet lake, maroon and pansy purple.

P. Peter Brand (p78)

And now, quite suddenly, the flower buds appear, tiny hard knobs on slender stems; they seem to form overnight but afterwards remain upheld for weeks without seeming change. Again all at once there is a further transformation; the plants increase greatly in size; the foliated spears have turned into small bushes, with leaves well spread; the plants are twice, three times the size they were a few days before; the buds are larger although still solid, hard and globular. *May has come!* They stay like this, still and beautiful to look at, and it seems as if a month or more must pass before any flowers can show, for how could a large peony blossom eight or nine inches across be developed in any shorter time from a hard ball the size of a marble? But we know better, and after a fortnight we visit them daily, until one morning a few of the buds near to bursting are showing little patches of yellowish white. The very next day, if it is warm and sunny, the third miracle has happened; *the first peony is out!* It is the flower of a single variety and has spread its broad, gleaming petals away from its golden heart, drinking in the sunshine. Others soon follow it, and a supreme moment arrives when the first of the double flowers appears, huge, majestic, and perfect. The golden month of June is well set, and the peony is the month's crown, the focus, and the highlight of all that is beautiful in the garden picture.

Many of our trees, shrubs and a few of our herbaceous perennials owe a great popularity to the cheerful and in some cases strikingly beautiful colours which their foliage assumes towards the decline of the year. Peonies have a claim to be included among these. The normal colour of their foliage when in flower is green of varied shades, and bronze. In some varieties however these greens change and run the whole gamut of browns, yellows and reds. Another friend of the boyhood paint-box, "Burnt sienna", is prominent and even a bright pink is sometimes to be seen. It is not certain to what extent seasons or soils influence this habit of changing the foliage colour towards autumn, but varieties which frequently display this tendency, are noted in the list.

Peonies have other claims to consideration besides their great and varied beauty in colour and form and their perfume. One of these is their permanence when once planted: another, their power of endurance through hardships such as extremes of climate and neglect, under which many other so-called "hardy" plants would fail in part or succumb altogether. Peonies bridge the season between spring and summer. Once properly planted there are no gaps to be filled at the end of the season; each plant settles in to stay, is a friend who becomes better known each succeeding year, and of the kind which improves on acquaintance. There are instances in my own experience of plants flowering in the same position, year after year, for seventy years; and there is no reason why they should not go on far longer in a good depth of soil. There is probably no hardy plant that gives such an abundant return for so little care. It was noticeable in many gardens which became wildernesses during the years of war that the peonies were the only garden plants left alive and in many cases they were still in fullest vigour when peace came and their owners returned home.

As a peony needs a square yard in which to become well established and exhibit its beauty to the full, room cannot be found for many in tiny gardens, but even the smallest plot should possess at least three or four. Mrs. Edward Harding, an American enthusiast, writes in her book on peonies, "No garden can really be too small to hold a peony. Had I but four square feet of ground at my disposal I would plant a peony in the centre, and proceed to worship. Owners of small gardens are often fearful of having insufficient room for this stately subject. I think they do not realize how much pleasure comes from the possession of even half a dozen plants, or three, or two, or just one." If this is true in respect of small gardens how loud is the call from larger gardens for a generous supply. Peonies should, therefore, be planted near at hand for close enjoyment of their beauty as well as in masses for distant colour effect, in lines straight or curving on the margins of shrubberies, and in groups between shrubs; in large and small beds in the midst of turf; in borders at the foot of walls, and in formal mixed borders at constant intervals. They should, in their less expensive kinds, be planted freely in open copses, and the rougher parts of the garden. All these situations they adorn.

P. Albâtre (p43)

The following, written many years ago by William Robinson, is interesting and valuable: "Most gardens contain spots so shaded that few plants will thrive in them. In such places peonies would grow luxuriantly; and their colour would often be more intense, while they would last much longer than if fully exposed to the sun. They may therefore be made useful as well as ornamental even in small pleasure grounds, although their proper place is undoubtedly the fronts of shrubberies and plantations and the sides of carriage drives. Where distant effect is required no plants answer so well, as their size and brilliancy render them striking even at a long distance. When planted on either side of a grass walk their effect is admirable, especially in the morning and about sunset; and when planted in masses they are invaluable for lighting up sombre nooks. The most brilliant and one of the boldest things in wild gardening is a group of scarlet peonies in meadow grass in early summer."

Drifts of peonies at Kelways Nursery, Langport

Wherever there is either full sunlight all the day or half-shade for a part of it; that is the place for peonies. Trees which allow sunlight to come through and which are not too greedy at the roots are good companions for them; i.e. flowering cherries, peaches, plums, and crab apples. Especially in respect of the paler varieties of peonies this half-shade preserves the individuality of the tints, which so subtly distinguish one variety from another. On the other hand trees such as elms, oaks, beeches, maples, and chestnuts, cast too heavy a shade and are too greedy at their roots to be recommended as near neighbours.

Those who have room could well plant quite large breadths of peonies as they have been in the habit of doing with azaleas, rhododendrons and roses. Highly coloured kinds of good habit look extremely well in the landscape, and it is the custom to use them extensively in this manner in the United States and Canada. They are as hardy as the dock, and do not require lime-free or any special kind of soil.

But perhaps the greatest joy to be obtained from the peony is from planting a well-chosen selection of single, double and semi-double kinds in a large bed or border and in examining their differences and savouring their varying loveliness at leisure. Additions can be made annually, selected from varieties seen at flower shows, in friends' gardens, in nurseries, or from descriptions in catalogues, until a really fine collection is achieved.

A peony garden, where the whole range of European, Chinese, Japanese, and Moutan forms may be gathered together to demonstrate unmistakably their charms, their surpassing grandeur, or their fragrance should certainly be worthwhile. Such a garden should not be arranged formally and the peonies may well have for their associates early-flowering daffodils or late-flowering lilies, something of a bulbous-rooted character before and after their coming, something to set off rather than to vie with them, thus making their abiding-place a greater attraction than it would otherwise be. In no case, however, should such accompaniments be overdone. Of course, it might well be urged that a comprehensive peony garden is only possible in very large gardens, and this, indeed, may be true. At the same time, there is room in most gardens for peony beds or borders, wherein a well-chosen selection can find place.

It is not generally known in this country that the herbaceous peony lends itself to the bringing on of early flowers in the greenhouse or conservatory, yet in America the plant is widely used for this purpose. It does well in tubs and in very large pots or planted out in greenhouse or conservatory beds. The true peony is also very easy to grow in a cold greenhouse; good-sized plants put into pots in the autumn will give flowers as beautiful as those produced in the open air. In order to advance the blooming by a month or two, it is only necessary for them to be put about January or February in a greenhouse with a moderate temperature, that is to say, about 55° to 60° Fahrenheit (12 to 16 Celsius).

As a cut flower, the peony, so beautiful, so fragrant, so impressive and long lasting, with its long firm stalks, is ideal for interior decoration; it is worth growing for this purpose alone. The flowers if gathered in the bud will open to their fullest extent in water and will retain their colour tones, some of which are apt to be lost in the full heat of a blazing sun. It is even true that flowers which have opened in water in the house exhibit more delicate variations of colour tones than if they had opened on the plants in full sun. They can also be cut when young and kept in cold storage for a long time in readiness for any particular date ahead for which they may be required. Cut in bud when the colour of the petals is only just showing, and the stems plunged in water for an hour or so, they will sustain a journey of two or three days by post or rail, and when again placed in water will open fully. Their fragrance remains fresh to the end and is not overpowering at close quarters. The flowers will retain their beauty and last longer in water if each day a small portion of the stem is cut off with a sharp knife and fresh water given. A reliable feminine authority tells me that, "to the busy woman of to-day they are the modern answer to the housewife's prayer for a decorative and easy flower arrangement". I think the single varieties are quite as beautiful. In fact many people admire them even more than the magnificently opulent double forms.

P. Cascade (p45)

Apart from garden and room decoration, peonies should be more extensively exhibited as cut flowers at early-summer flower shows. They are always the subject of admiration by the public, and if shown separately and correctly named, are certain of increasing the percentage of marks awarded to a group of hardy perennials for competition. In North America and Canada, shows devoted to peonies alone take place in June and July. Innumerable classes under various headings are arranged for competitive awards and so popular are peonies everywhere South and North, East and West that the entries are legion and spectacular shows result.

Even if peonies bore no flowers they would merit a place in the garden for the sake of their handsome foliage. All peonies produce bushes of ornamental foliage attractive in outline and veining, in varying metallic shades of green and bronze through the flowering period and I have spoken of the young stems of vivid carmine breaking through the soil in March and unfolding in April and May. In addition many varieties are resplendent again in the autumn in tints of gold, orange, scarlet, rose and purple brown. Beds of peonies in September and October can be as charming as flowering borders; the leaves are invaluable for house decoration and harvest festivals at a time when flowers are scarce.

CHAPTER II

The three groups of the peony family

Peonies may be divided roughly, from the amateur gardener's point of view, into three sections:

(a) The June-flowering varieties of *P. lactiflora* or "Chinese peonies". This is the most important section for the average garden.

(b) The various herbaceous species. These flower in May or earlier, certain of them are extremely desirable.

(c) Varieties of *P. suffruticosa* (*P. moutan*), the shrubby or "tree" peony, and hybrid varieties between it and the shrubby *P. delavayi* & *P. ludlowii*.

(a) To those who have only met with peonies such as the May-flowering old double crimson of gaudy colouring and not very pleasing perfume, the June-flowering varieties of *P. lactiflora* will be an astounding revelation. The singles so fine and pure in line and colour, the large doubles in such incomparably delicate tints as well as in handsome, brilliant colours and charming in their fragrance, and the "Imperials"; Japanese types, in the magnificence of their rich contrasting colours. There are still people who have never seen these June-flowering kinds. "We have always had peonies," said a gardening friend to me, "but I don't think they are up to much." When she made the acquaintance of a glorious group of new hybrids, she gasped with surprise. "These are not peonies!" she exclaimed. *Paeonia lactiflora*, the species from which the many beautiful single and double varieties originated, is described by botanists as follows: "Bearing white or pink flowers with petals two and a half to three inches (6-8cm) broad, sepals five to ten. Leaflets oblong, acute three to four inches (7.5-10cm) long, one to one and a half inches (2.5-4cm) broad, glabrous, bright green, often coloured red at the edges and with red veins. Lower leaves with about five segments in each of the three divisions. Stems two to three feet (60-90cm) long; often branched, bearing one to five flowers."

P. officinalis Rubra Plena, the "old double crimson" (p85)

The roots (which are said to be eaten by the Tatars of Mongolia) are hard and tough and branch from a harder central core. They are fusiform or spindle-shaped affairs, hard and fleshy, in appearance something between dahlia and rhubarb roots. This feature and the store of juices contained in a well-matured piece, explain why peonies will travel so safely and well to distant lands. These roots become, in time, as thick as a man's finger or even wrist, and will grow downwards to a depth of two feet (60cm).

"Doubling" takes place freely in the flowers of this as well as of some other species, by the evolution of the numerous stamens into petals. When it has only just started, we get varieties belonging to the so-called Japanese or "Imperial" section, with their extremely beautiful centres. At the half-developed stage the flowers are called semi-double; the petaloids are then often narrow to the point of being thread-like; when the change is complete we have the fully double kinds.

Raisers have taken advantage of this latent power of change to cross-fertilise and raise seedlings from which they have selected those showing the most striking variation for naming and distribution. This has for over a century been practised in France, for three-quarters of a century in England, and more recently in America. The naming of seedlings can be overdone, but there are at least several hundred named varieties mentioned in various catalogues, all more or less distinct and worth growing; a great many of them are beautiful beyond description. A list of those varieties which we consider amongst the most desirable, is given in Chapter V.

(b) The various herbaceous species of peony which flower in May or a little earlier are many, but are reduced in number if those that are nearly allied are brought together and those that have not great interest except to botanists or are not generally available, are excluded. *P. officinalis* is the largest section, and is represented throughout England, particularly in cottage gardens, by the old double red (*P. officinalis* Rubra Plena). As this is almost the only peony known to a great portion of the general public, many are apt to think of "peonies" in terms of this one kind, which is unfortunate. It provides a fine bit of colour for the short time it is in flower. It used to be popular in the West Country in the old days of "Club Walking" on May 29th, "Oak Apple Day", when its flower, like a small red cabbage, was prominent in the buttonholes of male members of the local Benefit Society. The double white and double rose varieties of *P. officinalis* are also attractive.

Some of the single-flowered relatives of *P. officinalis* are not particularly showy; they are low growing, their flowers are not large, nor numerous, and are chiefly rather dull in shades of mauve or red. The very notable ally of the *P. officinalis* group, *P. peregrina* and varieties of it, are unique in their astonishingly pure rosy scarlet colour.

There have been many attempts to cross-fertilise members of the *P. officinalis* section with the *P. lactiflora* kinds. As the former flower in May and the latter in June it has not been easy, but a few crosses have been made and distributed in this country and in America. They are spoken well of and may become popular when more widely known (See Chapter V).

P. peregrina (p86)

Of other May-flowering herbaceous species, two are outstanding: *P. mlokosewitschii* and *P. wittmanniana*. Both are imposing in leaf and flower, and they are yellow, a colour rare in herbaceous peonies. And there is the interesting small-flowered species, *P. veitchii* and its variety *P. veitchii* var. *woodwardii*.

P. veitchii (p86)

Apart from their obvious differences when growing, all these species differ widely botanically from *P. lactiflora*. For instance here is the description of *P. officinalis*: "Petals dark crimson, much imbricated, abovate one and a half to two inches (4-5cm) broad, stamens half an inch (1.2cm) long, anthers rather shorter, glabrous, paler beneath; the lowest with fifteen to twenty lanceolate acute confluent leaflets, one to two inches (2.5-5cm) broad." The roots are more tuberous in form than those of *P. lactiflora*; detached portions will form calluses and from these buds will sprout and produce plants, whereas *P. lactiflora* will only grow from portions which already possess an eye or stem bud near the crown of the plant.

(c) The tree peony is one of the noblest shrubs available for beds in the garden or for the border; it is extremely hardy, being subject to temperatures below zero Fahrenheit (-18 Celsius) in its native country. It flourishes in Britain in the open garden under the simplest treatment in almost any kind of soil. The smallest specimen will flower in the most astonishing manner, bearing magnificent blossoms often one foot (30cm) across and increase in size until it becomes a large shrub carrying a large number of flowers. The flowers are comparable in size, beauty or in range of colour, from the most delicate tints to those of strongest splendour, by those of any hardy plant or shrub. Tree peonies are a great ornament in gardens from the first days of spring on account of their elegant foliage, so beautiful in outline and colouring. Their enormous flowers open in April and May.

The most important tree peonies for gardens are the many hybrids and varieties of:

(i) *Paeonia suffruticosa* of Chinese, Japanese and French origin. These flower in April, May and June, and are superb when in flower and with attractive foliage. A few are scented. In many instances the magnificent blossoms are larger even than the largest of the herbaceous varieties.

(ii) The hybrid varieties resulting from crossing it with *Paeonia ludlowii,* a yellow-flowered species. These are mainly the result of the work in France of Lemoine et fils, and Professeur Louis Henry. They exhibit all shades of yellow, orange and bronzy red.

P. Claire de Lune (p79)

P. Dinner Plate (p55)

CHAPTER III

Where, when and how to plant

As I have already remarked, peonies of all kinds may be planted in any part of the garden where there is direct sunshine during some part of the day and a soil of average consistency and good depth, but not too near the roots of large trees. One preference is perhaps a sandy soil, well mulched from time to time, irrespective of whether it is an acid or limey, but it must be well drained, for stagnant moisture is fatal. They do especially well in a bed raised a foot above the path.

They are to be recommended for all the special purposes already mentioned and also for planting in the kitchen garden for cut flowers for the house. All the sections of the family are equally hardy; but in the south and west of Britain an unusually early spell of warmth in the spring sometimes causes a premature sprouting of buds which a subsequent frost or keen east wind may injure. This is more noticeable with the tree varieties and is an argument rather for an open situation than a sheltered one. There is no insuperable reason why all three groups, *P. lactiflora* and its varieties, herbaceous species and tree species and varieties should not be planted together in one bed or border. This would extend the flowering period from the end of April until July. They would be well arranged so that the tallest growers were in the middle of the bed or at the back of the border, and the June-flowering alternated with the earlier kinds. But the general wish may be for greater uniformity in kind and in time of flower, and to this end separate beds and borders for each section can be made. It is a matter of taste and convenience.

For the best effect it is probably advisable, where possible, to plant in groups of three or five or more of the same variety, rather than singly and, for the sake of contrast, to distribute the colours impartially throughout the bed or border, being careful to plant the lower growing kinds near the front. And unless it is intended to take up and plant elsewhere every other plant in three or four years' time, plenty of room should be given from the beginning. Peonies are a permanent investment and individual plants will form quite large clumps with reasonable encouragement. Given plenty of space and deep rich soil the size of the flowers is greatly increased and their colours intensified.

P. Duchesse de Nemours (p45)

Many subjects such as bulbs and dwarf alpines may be planted actually between and among peonies and, in beds and borders, given plenty of room, peonies associate well with delphiniums, gaillardias, *Lobelia cardinalis*, michaelmas daisies, etc., or in front of tall-growing plants. Gladioli, flowering when the peony blooms are long past, narcissi and scillas are amongst the most admirable of consorts for them. Shakespeare must have noticed the companionability of the lily, for he speaks of "thy banks with peonied and lilied brim" in *The Tempest*.

Of narcissi, those of the strong-flowering, trumpet section of golden colour are preferable. The narcissi will flower while the peonies are thrusting up their young carmine shoots. Later the peonies will expand their softly coloured, massive blooms, while, after their beauty has waned, the tall flower-spires of the stately lilies will gleam above the spreading foliage.

P. Sarah Bernhardt (p67)

In shrubberies and woodland the *P. officinalis* group and some of the strongest growers of the *P. lactiflora* section can be used, but in no more than half-shade and not if there is danger of their being starved by the roots of the shrubs and trees. The *P. officinalis* varieties are especially adaptable for growing in rough grass. Holes should be filled with good soil, and the grass not allowed to grow close to the plants for the first year, after which an annual clearing round the collar will be sufficient to enable the plants to hold their own with any native herbage that may appear.

For this country I consider that the very best time to move and replant is in September and October or the first convenient date after the ground has been made ready, but not later than the end of March. Some growers in America have declared that spring planting is even better than autumn. I do not think that the peony cares very much as long as it gets room for its toes when planted, and for expansion afterwards; naturally the longer it has in which to send out young root growth before the summer the better. It should also be borne in mind that they are early-season bloomers and are chary of producing flowers the first summer and it is better that they should wait until the second season before doing so. In any event the excellence and true character of the variety cannot justly be judged from the first season's flowers.

The best plants to obtain are roots of two or three years of age. They gp straight ahead and become established and flower satisfactorily sooner than old clumps or divisions of large clumps; the latter take much longer to send out fibrous roots and to re-establish themselves. Peonies, however small the plant, as long as there is an "eye", will sprout and grow; it is almost difficult to kill them; but they are impatient of removal after being planted.

The vitality of peony plants is so remarkable that there have been instances of plants arriving in mid-Canada from England in the autumn, placed in their frozen state in a cellar, and planted in the spring, not only surviving, but nourishing to perfection. Peonies, after two months' journey to New Zealand, arriving at Christmas, have shown through the soil a fortnight after being planted. I have seen small portions of roots cast away on a rubbish heap in the autumn, throwing up leaves and buds the next year although they had had no food except from their own fleshy tubers and from rain, sun and air.

When planting herbaceous peonies, whether species or garden varieties, a hole for each plant should be dug one to two feet (60cm) deep and one and a half feet (45cm) across. Where convenient it would be well, in the summer beforehand, to have the whole bed or border trenched, or at any rate deeply dug, and enriched by the incorporation of well-rotted farmyard manure, compost, or humus of some kind. If this cannot be done and the soil needs enrichment, manure or some other humus should be placed at the bottom of each hole at planting time and lightly covered with soil so that the roots will not actually touch it. Manure not really decomposed, or which still has straw in it, or detritus covered with white threads, must be avoided or the roots may become adversely affected. Not less than two feet (60cm), and, for the production of the largest flowers and for the best permanent effect, four feet (120cm), should be the distance from the nearest plant.

The *P. lactiflora* varieties and the various herbaceous species, should be planted so that the crown of the plant which produces the stem buds will not be more than one and a half to two inches (3.5-5cm) beneath the ordinary surface level. The planting should be completed by the soil being placed over their crowns. If the soil should heave or expand from frost it should be again lightly trodden, and the ground levelled by drawing away the raised or superfluous soil above the crown so that no more than two inches (5cm) remains above the crest of the plant. The reason for the recommendation that the ground should be deeply dug and well manured as long before the planting season as may be possible is in order to ensure that the plants may achieve and retain the highest standard for the indefinite number of years of which peonies are so outstandingly capable.

P. Nymphe (p58)

P. Shirley Temple (p51)

CHAPTER IV

The care of peonies

It is quite useless to give herbaceous peonies a covering in winter; it will be positively harmful through the lessening of the aeration of the soil and the beneficial action of the frost and snow, to both of which they are accustomed in their native habitat.

P. Jan van Leeuwen (p47)

In cases where roses are killed to the ground by severe winters, peonies survive. They defy storm, hail, hot wind and blizzard, and triumph over all. But although the peony is so extremely hardy, vigorous, persistent and enduring, it does not become a nuisance in the border by rambling or spreading unduly. It merely asks to be well started in life and left to itself to increase in strength and beauty. In the case of tree peonies, however, though they are extremely hardy, nevertheless in countries such as Britain where mild weather frequently occurs early in the year and is sometimes succeeded by a late frost just when flower buds are beginning to develop, it is prudent to give some slight protection during periods of variable temperature, in case these buds may become injured. If these elementary precautions are taken, there is no reason why peonies should not be suitable plants for exposed gardens with a harsh climate.

The cultivation of the ground and the keeping of it clean round and between the plants are in my opinion of more value in good soils than the application of mulches and fertilizers. A mulch each autumn however, will not be without reward on light soils. Some growers do not mulch but fork in bone meal or any other artificial manure that will not encourage growth of foliage rather than flower. Fertilisers rich in potash should be chosen but in moderate doses. Farmyard manure is excellent but must be kept well away from the plants. During periods of drought in the growing season it is advisable to water copiously twice a week; this is preferable to frequent or daily light watering. In keeping the ground clean between the plants, and this can only be done effectively between November and March, care must be taken not to interfere with the roots, as these spread almost horizontally as well as downwards.

As I have already stated, peonies which originate in North-Eastern Asia are so extremely hardy that they flourish all the better in the summer from resting through a long winter spell of frost and snow. This accounts for their giving such successful results in the Northern States of America and in Canada. *Paeonia emodi*, originating in Northern India, has a shorter sleep and is slightly "tender", that is to say the flower buds could be ruined by frost unless protected.

If planted in early autumn or in the spring, each plant should have the contents of a can of water poured round it after being planted and should not be allowed to get really dry at any time during its first summer. It is also better for the plants if they are not allowed to flower at all during the first season. The foliage should not be cut off until late in the autumn when it has begun to decay and then it should be severed near the ground to obviate any possible infection in the foliage from affecting the main plant.

One of the things the peony grower must learn is that the leaves must not be cut away until they have actually ripened, for they are necessary to the proper completion of growth and flowers of next year. But just after flowering the flower stems can be shortened in the interest of tidiness. When eventually the foliage is cut to the ground it should be taken away and burnt.

Supports are not necessary with the dwarfer varieties or in sheltered gardens, but in some more exposed situations with the taller kinds, as the flowers on established plants are so large and heavy, it is well to obviate the effect of strong gales, and the weight of heavy rains. The most suitable supports are medium-weight three-foot or four-foot (90-120cm) bamboo canes. Three or four of these stuck firmly into the ground with string round them are unobtrusive and are a satisfactory method of keeping the plant together, whereas large stakes are unsightly. The cartwheel shaped plastic or metal ring supports are also most satisfactory and efficient as they are all but invisible beneath the foliage.

To obtain the largest individual flowers for exhibitions, lateral buds may be removed when about the size of peas, but in my opinion the fullest natural beauty of the plants as an ornament to the garden is exhibited when all the buds are allowed to remain; this not only increases the number of flowers but also prolongs the flowering period. To many, these complete flower heads make even more artistic appeal than the massive central bloom alone: for example varieties like Kelway's Supreme with its saucer-shaped secondary blossoms, provide extremely attractive flower clusters.

P. Kelway's Supreme (p57)

Raising garden varieties of peonies from seed is almost entirely left to professional nurserymen. It is a long process and the quality of the flowers so produced is unpredictable. If, however, an amateur gardener wishes to raise plants from seed it is well to gather the seeds just as the pods are opening and before the seeds turn dark and hard. If sown at once in pots or pans indoors they will germinate fairly soon, but when hardened they take a year in soil before the seed case disintegrates and the germ can break through. The seedling plant will not reach the flowering stage for other three or four years.

Pests and diseases

It appears to be a custom in books on gardening to write a chapter in great detail about the numerous pests, which attack so many classes of plants. In my opinion this is so much overstressed that it is a wonder that amateurs embark on any gardening whatsoever! In regard to the peony, at one time it seemed safe to say there was nothing whatever that it had to fear, as neither insect nor vermin attacked it and even rabbits passed it by. Peonies as a matter of fact are so stout and vigorous and the roots are so hard and fleshy that it is difficult for those grubs, which are a nuisance to frailer kinds of plants, to make any inroads upon them, at any rate while the plants themselves are in a healthy state.

Pest and disease prevention and control (2013)

Peonies are indeed tough; they are never troubled by rabbits or deer, or by any of the smaller pests such as aphids, spider mites, whitefly or scale insects. Ants will take away the sticky sugars exuded by developing flower buds. If they did not, the buds might glue together and open unevenly, so here is a classic example of symbiosis, whereby both plant and beast benefit from each other.

During the spring, developing shoots may suddenly wilt. This is due to *Botrytis paeoniae*. At the base of the wilted shoot will be seen brown lesions often showing grey spore growth. Any shoots wilting like this must be removed immediately and destroyed, and a close eye kept on the plant in subsequent days. The best way to keep plants healthy and free of disease is to maintain good air movement around each plant, particularly at the base, and to cut off all of the old foliage at the end of the season and destroy. If these shoots are not removed, the botrytis may reach back into the roots and persist from year to year, gradually weakening the plant.

Ants at work!

Sometimes in late summer, leaf spots may appear on the mature peony leaves, this is usually due to *Cladosporium* infecting the plant. Remove the old foliage at the end of the season and the problem is unlikely to persist in the following year, provided good air movement is maintained around the plants.

CHAPTER V

The best June-flowering peonies

To compile a list of the most desirable of the many named varieties of herbaceous June-flowering peonies requires a long acquaintance with them. Not only the beauty of the flower, but the habit of growth, free-flowering quality and the consistently high standard of each individual kind in successive seasons has to be considered.

I have been fortunate in having been in actual personal touch with an immensely varied collection during a long lifetime. For more than half a century I have spent many hours of many days from the end of May to the beginning of July examining hundreds of named garden varieties of French, English, Japanese, and lately, American origin. If I were challenged as to which of all these I myself would plant in order to form an unrivalled collection, I would select from the following list.

Those I mention have stood the test of time and competition. Kinds difficult to obtain are omitted, and also a few varieties which appear to be outstanding, but which are so new that there has not yet been time to prove them properly.

For convenience I have arranged the selection in relation to the colour of the flowers. It has not been easy, as some kinds alter slightly between the opening stages and maturity, or even according to the age or vigour of the plant itself, or from seasonal climatic conditions. I have marked specially the singles (*S*) and the so-called "Imperials" (single-flowered Japanese type with large bosses of petaloids) (*J*) and the semi-doubles (*SD*). It will be observed that information is also given as to anything unusual in relation to height, fragrance, and flower profusion, autumn colour in the foliage, and the comparative earliness or lateness of the flowering period.

P. Bunker Hill (p69)

P. Karl Rosenfield (p73)

Here is my list, preceded by notes as to the meaning of the abbreviations used:

Abbreviations

S	Single flowered
J	Single flowered, but with a central boss of petaloids of yellow, in some cases edged crimson. Japanese type, also known as imperial form
SD	Semi-double, i.e. with loosely arranged inner petals sometimes of narrow or even threadlike form, and often with golden anthers showing at the centre of or between the petals
D	Fully double
VE	Beginning to flower the last week of May
E	Commencing to flower early in June
M	In flower in mid-June
L	In flower late in June
VL	Can sometimes linger on into July

AGM   The Royal Horticultural Society's Award of Garden Merit

Names in brackets are those of the raisers with the date when they were raised.

Height: Depends so much on location and the soil, but as a general rule most lactiflora peonies will attain around 80-95cm (33-38ins). Shorter ones will be from 60-80cm (24-32ins), and taller cultivars 95-120cm (39-48ins).

Quotes in italics are James Kelway's own words from the original book, or from his nursery notes.

An asterisk denotes plants not known to or mentioned by James Kelway at the time the original book was written, which have been added to the listing to update it.

White

Albâtre (D) (Crousse 1880). *"White double, of perfect form. Charming sweet fragrance."* Not readily available but worth a search. (M). **(illus p15)**

Alice Harding (D) (Lemoine 1921). *"A lovely tint of palest amber on white ground, eventually turning wholly white. Very large and massive, but occasionally semi-double. Incurved centre. Delicately beautiful. Vigorous and tall."* (E).

Argentine (D) (Lemoine 1924). *"Creamy white globular flowers of superb shape."* Very fragrant. A late flowering peony, which is shorter growing to around 80cm. (L).

Baroness Schroeder (D) (Kelway 1888). *"Pale flesh-white tinted cream, turning snow-white. Very large flowers, and handsome foliage. Rose scented. One of the most beautiful double whites for colour, shape and mass effect. The flowers last well and are even finer when cut and in water than in the garden."* This perhaps one of Kelways' finest introductions and is grown the world over for commercial cut flower production. (M). **(illus p44)**

Boule de Neige (D) (Calot 1867). One of the oldest cultivars of *P. lactiflora*. Large broad, semi-double flowers, opening blush pink, but then fading gracefully to milky white. A rewarding variety for cutting with long strong stems and plentiful side buds. (M). **(illus p44)**

*Bowl of Cream (D) (Klehm 1963). Very large bowl shape double flowers. They are a gorgeous creamy white with a yellow hue to the central petals. This peony is robust growing with bright green foliage and the blooms are very weather resistant despite their size. They have the sweetest scent. Mid to late flowering. (M-L). **(illus p44)**

P. Baroness Schroeder (p43)   *P. Bowl of Cream (p43)*

P. Boule de Neige (p43)

Canarie (D) (Guerin 1861). *"Creamy white with a light yellow centre. Carpels tipped pink."* A fragrant and beautiful taller variety. Takes a while to establish but is a complete joy ultimately. (M). **(illus p46)**

Cascade (D) (Kelway, date unknown). This is one of the most magnificent of all peonies. Huge flowers, palest blush on opening, turning pure white. Thread like filament centre, with large and broad outer guard petals. Taller growing with very robust stems that do not need staking. Later flowering. (VL). **(illus p19)**

*Charlie's White (D) (Klehm 1951). Large bomb shaped flowers, which have broad guard petals surrounding a raised mound. The central petals have a yellow tint giving a golden glow to the depths of the flower. This is a vigorous peony with the flowers produced on strong stems that rarely need staking; as such it is a very popular cut flower commercially. Sweet fragrance. (M). **(illus p46)**

Duchesse de Nemours AGM (D) (Calot 1856). *"Sulphur or light canary yellow to pure white. Green carpels. Medium-sized flower, sometimes large. Fine foliage. Extremely sweetly scented. Useful as a cut flower."* Perhaps the best known white peony, and deservedly one of the most popular. Early flowering, with the most joyful of scents. (E). **(illus p29)**

Edith Cavell (D) (Kelway 1916). *"Milk-white with some bright yellow petals and red stain. Very sweet and large, delightful."* These large flowers, irregularly stained with red flecks have a delightful fragrance. Shorter growing. (M). **(illus p46)**

Festiva Maxima AGM (D) (Miellez 1851). *"Pure icy white with an occasional red blotch."* Unusually a double white peony without any trace of pink. A full double of fine size and shape. Taller growing plants which usually benefit from staking. (M). **(illus p9)**

P. Canarie (p45)   *P. Charlie's White (p45)*

P. Edith Cavell (p45)

P. Florence Nichols (p47)

*Florence Nichols (D) (Nichols 1938). Large fully double flowers, much like Sarah Bernhardt, but rather paler in tone. "*Although the blooms open blush pink, they soon pale around the edges to pure white. Excellent for cutting.*" (M). **(illus p46)**

*Gardenia (D) (Linns 1955). A most gorgeous full white double. The buds open palest blush pink but this colour quickly disappears in sunshine. The blooms have elegant form and the flowers have the sweetest fragrance, just like its namesake shrub. (M). **(illus p48)**

James Kelway (SD) (Kelway 1900). "*Blush-white changing to milk-white with golden glow at centre. Very large flowers of exquisite quality and perfect form. Very fragrant. Especially useful as a cut flower. Vigorous and rather tall. Good foliage. Second only to Kelway's Glorious for perfect beauty. Has been recorded as producing as many as sixty blooms to one plant.*" 'One of the grandest peonies known. It has grown for me an upstanding vigorous stem between four and five feet in height, crowned with a group of five or six flowers of most enchanting beauty. It has a quality of petal, which has no equal. It has the colour of untouched white, and a habit of remaining only half open for a long time, when cut in the bud and kept from direct sunlight.' From *Peonies in the Little Garden*, by Mrs. Edward Harding. This is a truly awesome peony and also one of the very tallest. Do not attempt to grow without staking! (L). **(illus p48)**

*Jan van Leeuwen (J) (Van Leeuwen 1928). Milky white guard petals with a beautiful golden centre. The individual flowers take on an almost wax like appearance. Fragrant and very free flowering. This peony is unusual in that it lacks the red pigmentation in the leaves, which emerge bright green making it unmistakable in the border. (M). **(illus p34)**

Kelway's Glorious (D) (Kelway 1908). "*The finest of all double white peonies. Ravishingly lovely. Gleaming white with creamy glow in the depths. Crimson streaks outside the guard petals. Wonderful perfection of* form; deep funnel-shaped centre of incurving petals with broad widely spread rings of surrounding petals, immense flower six to seven inches across. Strongly scented of roses. Plant of medium height of first-rate habit with stout stems and dark green foliage. The flowers are freely produced and last well when cut. Blooms every year on every stem." Admired worldwide for a hundred years. This peony does need time to establish before its true majesty is revealed. (L). **(illus below)**

P. Gardenia (p47)

P. James Kelway (p47)

P. Kelway's Glorious (p47)

*Krinkled White (S) (Brand 1928). Really beautiful flowers of simple form. The pure white petals open with a faint blush and are lightly crimped like a butterfly's unfurling wings. Golden centres; a distinct peony in the border. Good bushy habit and plants rarely need staking. (M). **(illus below)**

P. Krinkled White (p49)   *P. Marie Lemoine (p49)*

Laura Dessert AGM (D) (Dessert 1913). *"Creamy-white guard petals with bright canary yellow centre. Snow-white with primrose base to petals when mature. Large full double. Medium height. The yellowest double peony."* (M).

Madame Edouard Doriat (D) (Doriat 1924). *"Cream-white to pure white, light carmine blotch at the centre. A beautiful globe-shaped flower with rounded petals. One flower per stem on long stiff stems. Lovely."* A taller growing peony, which excels as a cut flower. (L)

Marie Lemoine (D) (Calot 1869). *"White, cream at centre. Very large, sweetly scented."* This classic nineteenth century peony is still adored 144 years later. Similar to Duchesse de Nemours, but possibly a little more yellow in the centre of the bloom. The sweetly scented flowers are particularly good for cutting. A later flowering variety, which is also shorter growing so it rarely needs staking. (L). **(illus above)**

P. Mother's Choice (p51)

P. Primevère (p51)

P. Solange (p51)

*Mother's Choice (D) (Glasscock 1950). One of the best peonies for cutting. Very large creamy white flowers; a few petals will have some red streaks. Blooms are wonderfully fragrant and long lasting. The plants have glossy green leaves and strong stems that rarely need staking. (L). **(illus p50)**

Primevère (D) (Lemoine 1907). *"Blush-white with bright lemon-yellow petaloid centre which changes to milk white. When young, second only to Laura Dessert for yellowness. Sweetly scented."* This wonderful peony will delight again later in the year with worthy autumn colour. (M-L). **(illus p50)**

*Shirley Temple (D) (Origin unknown). Large double flowers open the palest blush pink, and quickly change to white. Exceptional quality of bloom. Mid to late flowering. Strong stems, and robust plants that rarely need staking. Excellent autumn colour. This is one of the most highly recommended of all peonies for garden performance. (M-L). **(illus p11,33)**

Solange (D) (Lemoine 1907). *"Cream or pale amber, sometimes with a pale orient-pink centre. Unique colour and lovely form. Dark green foliage."* This popular peony has the added bonus of being very late flowering. It is always one of the most highly recommended. (VL). **(illus p50)**

*Vogue (D) (Hoogendoorn 1949). An extremely beautiful, large double bloom of excellent form. The flowers open the merest blush pink and turn to white. Very fragrant. (M). **(illus p52)**

White Rose of Sharon (D) (Kelway 1886). *"Pure glistening white flowers with acutely reflexed petals and a prominent central tuft of bright yellow petaloids. Unique in shape."* Taller growing variety. (M).

*White Wings (S) (Hoogendoorn 1949). An extremely beautiful single, with pure white blooms. Yellow centre with red carpels. Very fragrant and free flowering. Mid season, shorter growing variety, with the flowers standing well in inclement weather. Very good autumn colour. (M). **(illus p52)**

P. Vogue (p51)

P. White Wings (p51)

Flesh pink and light rose

Albert Crousse (D) (Crousse 1893). *"Delicate shell-pink, a most attractive colour. Carmine flakes at centre. Globe-shaped flowers of medium size."* A classic peony that flowers profusely on strong stems with attractive foliage that colours well in the autumn. Late flowering. (L). **(illus p54)**

*Angel Cheeks (D) (Klehm 1975). Large and opulently blowsy blooms, which are clear pale pink, with large guard petals cupping a raised centre of fluffy petals. Rows of pale yellow stamens form a middle ring towards the centre of the flower. Mid season flowering, and shorter growing so rarely needs staking. (M). **(illus p54)**

*Catherina Fontijin (D) (Van der Valk 1952). A classic garden peony with large and broad blooms. The buds are slow to open, teasing you with the promise of the wonderful sight to come. They open palest pink, and pale to pure white whilst retaining a hint of blush pink in the centre. There is an inner ring of short golden stamens around a small tuft of central petals. These beautiful flowers are sweetly scented, and exceptionally good for cutting. Mid season. Taller variety. (M). **(illus p54)**

Claire Dubois (D) (Crousse 1886). *"Clear satiny rose-pink and silver. Fine incurved rose shape. Very large. Especially useful as a cut flower. Handsome dark foliage."* One of the great Victorian peonies. (M). **(illus p54)**

*Cornelia Shaylor (D) (Shaylor 1919). A classic and wonderful garden peony, superb for cutting. Large blooms with broad blush pink guard petals form a bowl holding a great mound of pale pink inner petals. A sophisticated and free flowering peony with a light sweet fragrance. Mid season. (M). **(illus p54)**

P. Albert Crousse (p53)   P. Angel Cheeks (p53)

P. Catherine Fontijin (p53)   P. Claire Dubois (p53)

P. Cornelia Shaylor (p53)

*Dinner Plate (D) (Klehm 1968). A glorious peony with enormous soft pink flowers. The larger outer petals have a silky paler edge. Pale yellow stamens peek through the central petals. Robust growing plants with thick strong stems. Late season flowering. (L). **(illus p27)**

*Fairy's Petticoat (D) (Klehm 1970). This outstanding hybrid has blowsy fully double blooms that are a delicate blush pink with a rich golden glow in their centre. The flowers fade softly to cream as they age. Great for cutting, the flowers have a light scent that can be enjoyed indoors. A very rewarding garden plant, mid season flowering. (M). **(illus p56)**

Germaine Bigot (SD) (Dessert 1902). *"Flesh-white shaded salmon colour, carmine flakes in centre. Very large loose crown-type flower showing golden anthers. Spicy fragrance."* The flowers can be huge on a well-grown plant; their beauty can take your breath away. Good foliage with excellent autumn colour. Long flowering period. (E-L).

Joy of Life (SD) (Kelway 1912). *"Smooth broad petals on spreading open flowers of very delicate blush pink. Enormous flowers of translucent beauty. One of the best peonies. Very sweetly scented. Flowers 10 ins across."* This astonishing peony is once seen and never forgotten. Although technically semi double the effect is of a huge single peony with multiple rows of petals. (M). **(illus p120)**

Kelway's Lovely (D) (Kelway 1905). *"Bright salmon rose, touched with cream pink. Central rose coloured tuft. Very large massive handsome flower."* One of the best of all the full doubles. The blooms take on an amazing transition from the moment the buds open, and the final flower bears little resemblance to the one that breaks free from the bud. Long flowering period. (E-L). **(illus p56)**

P. Fairy's Petticoat (p55)

P. Kelway's Lovely (p56)

Kelway's Supreme (D) (Kelway 1891). *"Delicate blush turning white, cup-shaped blooms with broad petals. Side flowers, freely produced, and are single or semi-double. Huge flowers, borne in clusters, when established. Vigorous, and continually in flower early to well into July. The very best of our productions of this type and colour. Excellent autumn colour."* Not readily available and takes time to establish, but a majestic plant to grace the garden. (E-VL). **(illus p37)**

Lady Alexandra Duff AGM (SD) (Kelway 1891). *"Delicate, gay, blush-pink turning paler, with carmine blotches on some central petals. Very large broad petalled flowers borne in clusters. Side flowers are single to semi-double of saucer shape with gold anthers. A handsome plant. One of the very finest of all peonies for exhibition and garden, and continuously in flower."* Highly alluring fragrance on this most magnificent of peonies. (E-L). **(illus below)**

P. Lady Alexandra Duff (p57)

*Moonstone (D) (Murawska 1943). Perhaps one of the most exquisite of all peonies, and one renowned for cutting. Broad double flowers which open blush pink and ultimately pale to pure white. If grown in a little shade the flowers retain their pink hue for longer. Sweetly scented. (M).

Monsieur Jules Elie AGM (D) (Crousse 1888). *"Light lavender-pink with silvery sheen changing to near white. Huge ball-shaped flower with very large outside petals. Varies in colour and shape as it matures. Useful for cut flowers. Very fragrant."* Stout but lax stems will usually benefit from staking. Always one of the most popular garden peonies. The raised centre of the flowers varies in colour and shape as the bloom develops. Distinct broad green foliage that is a particularly bright shade of green. One of the last peonies to flower, so it is very useful in extending the peony season. A shorter variety growing but usually best staked because the flowers are so heavy. (VL). **(illus p59)**

*Myrtle Gentry (D) (Brand 1925). This wonderful blush coloured double peony is considered by many to be one of the best of all. Shades of white suffused with tints of salmon and pink. Beautiful sweet fragrance. Free flowering over a long period. (E-L). **(illus p59)**

Noemi Demay (D) (Calot 1867). *"Tenderest pale blush white, with red carpels in the centre. Perfect form and purity and compact habit. Perhaps the showiest and earliest double."* This exceptional peony is also one of the shortest at around 50cm. (VE). **(illus p59)**

Nymphe (S) (Dessert 1913). *"Lively flesh-pink, golden centre. Large flowers."* Good autumn colour. Pretty flowers of apple blossom pink which are delightfully fragrant. A free flowering peony, which quickly forms a sturdy plant, smothered with blooms. This later flowering variety does particularly well in a shady part of the garden. (M). **(illus p33)**

P. Monsieur Jules Elie (p58)   *P. Myrtle Gentry (p58)*

P. Noemi Demay (p58)

P. Pillow Talk (p61)   *P. Raspberry Sundae (p61)*

P. Reine Hortense (p61)

P. Sorbet (p61)

*Pillow Talk (D) (Klehm 1973). Blowsy and voluminous. Large creamy pink double blooms with a heady fragrance. Great for cutting, and the winner of many awards. (M). **(illus p59)**

*Raspberry Sundae (D) (Klehm 1968) Large bomb shaped double blooms. The whole flower changes shape and size as it matures but is a multi-shaded mass of pink petals, some narrow and some broad. The central mound of petals tends to be the most deep in shade. Very heady fragrance. Mid season, shorter growing variety. (M). **(illus p59)**

Reine Hortense (S) (Calot 1857). *"Pale pink splashed crimson. Large compact flowers."* Very free flowering. One of the oldest peonies in cultivation, yet still one of the most endearing. A sensational flower of the palest rose pink. The colour is incredibly uniform and is minutely splashed on a white underlay. The centre of the flower is prominently flecked with crimson. This a very good peony for cutting, the fragrant blooms lasting for ages in a vase. Quite late flowering. (L). **(illus p60)**

*Sorbet (D) (Klinkhamer 1987). Large bomb shaped double blooms. The whole flower changes shape and size as it matures but is a multi-shaded mass of pink petals, some narrow and some broad. The colour of the central mound of petals tends to be the most deep in shade. Very heady fragrance. Mid season, shorter growing variety. (M). **(illus p60)**

Pink, rose, or deep salmon-pink

Auguste Dessert (SD) (Dessert 1920). *"Bright salmon-rose, edged silver. Distinct colour, pretty buds."* This peony is a unique salmon colour, intense in the centre of the flower and paling to a silver edge. Later flowering. (L). **(illus p62)**

P. Auguste Dessert (p61)

P. Bowl of Beauty (p64)

Beatrice Kelway (J) (Kelway 1905). *"Vivid pure rose outer petals, central petaloids rose, tipped and edged fawn and gold. Very striking and beautiful. A very tall vigorous plant with stout stems."* One of the most unique of all peonies if only for its perilously tall stems which can be as much as 5ft (150cm). (M-VL).

P. Big Ben (p64)

P. Emma Klehm (p65)

P. Doreen (p65)

*Big Ben** (D) (Auten 1943). Somewhat surprisingly an American hybrid! The flowers are deepest fuchsia pink, large dome shaped blooms with a crested top framed by a ring of larger horizontal petals. Highly scented, this is not a shy plant. (M). **(illus p63)**

Bowl of Beauty AGM (J) (Hoogendoorn 1943). *"Pale pink, with upright creamy white petaloids."* One of the most famous of all peonies and deservedly so. Upright lemony cream, ribbon-like petaloids fill the large bowl shaped flower formed by the bright pink guard petals. A strikingly lovely fragrant peony for the flower border, which will never disappoint. Mid to late flowering. (M-L). **(illus p62)**

P. Dr. Alexander Fleming (p64)

*Dr. Alexander Fleming** (D) (Origin unknown) A cross between Sarah Bernhardt and Bunker Hill. Large full deep pink double. Some stamens appear as the flower matures. Sweetly scented. Robust plants that rarely require staking. Freely produced side buds extend the flowering period so that this charming peony may still be in flower right at the end of June. Short dense bushy habit with good foliage. (M-L). **(illus p64)**

*Doreen (J) (Sass 1949). One of the most reliable of the Japanese style peonies, this cultivar has fuchsia pink guard petals with a rich centre of rosy pink staminodes, which have golden tips. Later flowering. (L). **(illus p63)**

Edulis Superba (D) (Lemoine 1824). *"Clear rosy-lilac, silvered."* Ancient cultivar, which still has a place in the border as a useful cut flower. Good fragrance. (VE-M).

*Emma Klehm (D) (Klehm 1951). A fully double peony with large heather pink flowers which pale more quickly on the sunny side of the flower, with the colour remaining through to the depths on the shady side. An extremely late flowering plant, in colour until the end of June. Shorter growing. (VL). **(illus p63)**

*Etched Salmon (D) (Klehm 1981). A lively peony with deep salmon pink to coral pink flowers, which have an etched edge. Extremely elegant in form and poise. It forms an attractive garden plant with flowers freely produced. Lovely fragrance. (M).

Evening World (J) (Kelway 1928). *"Lilac-pink outer petals with a deep cushion of flesh tint. Very fine and large."* One of Kelways' finest introductions. The large flat blooms have a clear white edging. As the pink centre of the petals gradually pales the whole flower turns white, emphasizing the bright green carpels. (M).

*Gilbert Barthelot (SD) (Doriat 1931). Semi double with large magenta pink blooms. The flowers often have a second set of petals in the centre, with a ring of golden stamens between. Fragrant blooms held atop strong stems, side buds freely produced. (M).

Globe of Light (J) (Kelway 1927). *"Lovely vivid pure rose colour with an enormous pure gold centre. Large blooms with green carpels."* Very majestic blooms, produced on a vigorous plant with good autumn foliage. (M-VL).

Kelway's Brilliant (J) (Kelway 1928). *"Pure carmine-red with shadings approaching scarlet; unique in colour. Crested centre."* Whilst not the largest blooms, their colour is like no other. A sort of psychedelic pinky-red that shimmers with an almost blue tint. (M-L). **(illus p111)**

P. Mr. G. F. Hemerik (p67)

*Lilac Time (J) (Lins 1958). Lilac pink guard petals make a bowl which cups the thinner central petals which form a billowing cushion of lilac white petaloids. The centre of the flower almost resembles a sea anemone! A lovely hue, which is quite an unusual shade for peonies Generally mid season flowering. (M).

*Mr. G. F. Hemerik (J) (Van Leeuwen 1930). Lipstick pink petals with a bright centre of saffron yellow petaloids. The dark glossy leaves are distinctly ribbed. This is a fine and late flowering peony. A wonderful garden plant with some of the best foliage of any peony. (L) **(illus p66)**

Nellie (S) (Kelway 1904). *"Brilliant pink changing to soft pink. Flowers borne in clusters. Probably the largest coloured single. Mint-like fragrance. Vigorous and tall."* One of the finest pink single peonies highly sought after. (E).

Rose of Delight (S) (Kelway 1925). *"A very brilliant clear pink, edged and marked with white. Handsome pure gold centre. Most striking and beautiful large flowers."* Tall upright grower. (E-L).

*Santa Fé (J) (Auten 1937). A highly unusual cultivar of Japanese origins. Mauve pink guard petals cup an inner centre of white petaloids. A most striking and colourful combination. Early to midseason flowering, this is a really good garden plant. (E-M). **(illus p68)**

Sarah Bernhardt AGM (D) (Lemoine 1906). *"Fine intense apple-blossom pink; each petal tipped silver. Very large handsome rose-type flower with pleasant scent. Good foliage. Fine for exhibition and as a cut flower."* This spectacular peony is one of the best loved and popular the world over, and has featured in millions of bridal floral arrangements. Quite tall growing, it often performs best with some support. Late flowering, so an ideal plant to extend the season. (L-VL). **(illus p30, 68)**

Van Dyck (D) (Crousse 1879). *"Outer and central petals pure mauve, mingled with creamy pink petals in the centre. Very fragrant. Large and fine."* An exceptionally elegant peony. (M). **(illus p69)**

P. Sante Fé (p67)

P. Sarah Bernhardt (p67)

P. Van Dyck (p67)

Deep carmine or cherry red

*Blaze (S) (Fay 1973). Impressive single blooms of brightest scarlet red, with glowing bright golden centres. The flowers are held on strong stems and sway gently in the slightest breeze. Mid season. (M). **(illus p70)**

*Bunker Hill (D) (Hollis1906). Large double blooms of bright Tyrian rose. The flowers are fragrant and freely produced. One of the later varieties to flower. (L). **(illus p41)**

Félix Crousse AGM (D) (Crousse 1881). *"Bright deep carmine red, silvered. Compact bomb type, incurved petals. Very large blooms, in clusters. Specially useful for cut flowers."* One of the most popular varieties in this colour range. A strong colour, the plants themselves are dense and bushy with lustrous dark foliage. (M-VL). **(illus below)**

P. Blaze (p69)   *P. Félix Crousse (p69)*

General McMahon (Syn. Augustin d'Hour) (SD) (Calot 1867). *"Deep solferino-red. Globe shaped. Very large."* Excellent peony, which is free flowering even as a young plant. Strong rich scent. (M-VL).

*Inspecteur Lavergne (D) (Doriat 1924). Large crimson red globe shaped flowers, often with white rims. Spicy fragrance. Free flowering, mid season. (M). **(illus below)**

P. Inspecteur Lavergne (p70)

*Kansas (D) (Bigger 1940). Large fully double blooms of deep fuchsia purple, or watermelon red. Excellent free flowering variety, great for cutting with strong straight stems and a rich heady fragrance. Mid season (M). **(illus below)**

P. Kansas (p71)

Kelway's Majestic (J) (Kelway 1928). *"Deep vivid cherry-red guard petals with a mass of long narrow ochre-yellow inner petals turning lilac and variously silvered or gilded. Very large."* One of Kelways' most magnificent peony successes. The cultivar has enormous vigour and establishes quickly to form large bushes. Really free flowering over a long period. (E-VL).

King of England (J) (Kelway 1901). A relatively little known peony. *"Deep red with carmine petaloids edged gold. Extremely handsome. Very large. Red stems."* A wonderful specimen peony for the border, which is vigorous and free flowering. (E-M)

*Many Happy Returns (D) (Hollingsworth 1986). A really fantastic new peony, which will ultimately become a popular commercial cut flower as propagation increases. Large bomb shaped flowers of a rich warm red. The stems are thick and long, and the blooms last a long time in water. Early to mid season flowering (E-M).

Mistral (S) (Dessert 1902). *"Deep velvety cherry colour with lighter edges, golden stamens."* Very fine peony of good substance, which stands the weather very well. (E-M). **(illus below)**

P. Mistral (p72)

*Nippon Beauty (J) (Auten 1927). This is a beautiful imperial peony, with deep red guard petals and a centre of red petaloids tipped and edged all round with gold. Very striking, it would form a wonderful focal point in the June border. Robust garden plants, flowering mid season. (M). **(illus p73)**

Othello (S) (Dessert 1908). *"Bright cherry-carmine. Upright habit."* An early flowering single peony with exceptionally bright flowers. (E). **(illus below)**

P. Nippon Beauty (p72)   *P. Othello (p73)*

Crimson and purplish red

Emperor of Russia (D) (Delache 1856). *"Deep rich amaranthine-purple shaded crimson."* A very handsome and free flowering peony. Although the flowers are not large, the intense coloration makes each individual flower glow. Long flowering period. (E-L).

Her Majesty (J) (Kelway 1925). *"Bright red, saffron-yellow filaments striped carmine. A fine rich deep colour and a huge flower."* An exquisite cultivar with very large plate sized blooms that resemble the most exotic water lily. (M).

Karl Rosenfield (D) (Rosenfield 1908). *"Purple red with petaloids. Good solid flower. Flowers on into July."* Very bright globe shaped flowers of purple red. Free flowering on strong stems with fine foliage. A good garden variety, which produces excellent blooms for cutting. (L). **(illus p41)**

President Poincaré (SD) (Kelway, date unknown). *"Rich pure ruby-crimson. Spice scented. Well formed incurved flower."* Large beautiful flowers with an alluring spicy scent. Midseason to later flowering. (M-L).

P. Sir Edward Elgar (p74)

Sir Edward Elgar (S) (Kelway 1905). *"Brightest maroon or chocolate crimson, a distinct shade."* A most rewarding peony with large deep rich blooms. Allow time to establish, after which it is a perennial joy. Long flowering season. (E-L). **(illus above)**

Dark maroon-red

Adolphe Rousseau (D) (Dessert & Mechin 1890). *"Fine lustrous maroon-red; a splendid colour. Very large. Dark foliage."* Double flowers with intensely deep cardinal red petals that have a satin like texture. Yellow stamens peep discreetly through the petals. An upright growing variety with deep green foliage and red stems, it is one of the best peonies of this colour for all round garden performance. The flowers have a slight scent. Mid to late flowering, this is a classic Victorian peony with perfect garden charm. (M-L). **(illus p75)**

P. Adolphe Rousseau (p74)

*Buckeye Belle (SD) (Mains 1956). This deep blood red very early flowering semi double peony from the United States has become widely known and a clear favorite. The colour is a bold red without any hint of pink, and the golden stamens peek out from among the petals. Flowering will often be in the middle of May. May be as tall as 90cm, but rarely needs staking. (E). **(illus p76)**

P. Buckeye Belle (p75)

P. Instituteur Doriat (p77)

P. Dr. H. B. Barnsby (p77)

Chocolate Soldier (S) (Auten 1939). A famous peony more for its name than anything else. *"Very dark chocolate purple with varnished sheen."* Quite small flowers. This peony does take time to establish but has a certain charm when in flower. The colour of the flowers is like no other peony. (M).

Dr. H. B. Barnsby (D) (Dessert 1913). *"Brilliant maroon-purple. A fine late flowering variety."* Rich deep flowers sit perfectly on top of dark lustrous foliage. The leaves are distinctly ribbed making it easy to identify. Late flowering. (L). **(illus p76)**

Instituteur Doriat (J) (Doriat 1925). *"Velvety carmine edged white. Large and distinct."* A most magnificent and dominating peony in a hue of deep velvety maroon. The centre of the flower consists of a tuft of narrow petaloids, which are forked at the ends and finely tipped with white. An extremely strong **grower**, soaring to over 100cm tall, sometimes benefitting from some support, although it is usually fine unaided. Later flowering cultivar. (L). **(illus p76)**

Lord Kitchener (S) (Kelway 1907). *"Intense maroon-red flowers; scarlet in sunlight. Borne in clusters. Extremely dark stems. The finest early red single peony."* Vigorous growing, and stunning in flower. (VE-E). **(illus below)**

Monsieur Martin Cahuzac (D) (Dessert 1899). *"Dark maroon-crimson with blackish sheen; a fine colour. Incurved semi-rose type, showing gold anthers."* Difficult to find and takes a while to establish, but one of the deepest of all red peonies. Free flowering over an extended period. (E-L).

P. Lord Kitchener (p77)   *P. William F. Turner (p78)*

Peter Brand (D) (Seit 1937). *"Fine deep shining red."* A really sumptuous peony and one of the best of this hue. Deep ruby red double flowers that become purple as they mature. Dark and lustrous foliage, which adopts rich tints in the autumn. The flowers are held on strong stems, and are excellent for cutting. This is a taller growing variety but is robust and rarely needs staking. Mid season, but flowering over a long period. (M). **(illus p12)**

Philippe Rivoire (D) (Riviere 1911). *"Deep amaranthine purple or maroon-red with black sheen. Fine form. Medium size. The only red peony with a tea rose scent. Medium height. Good foliage."* Whilst not the largest individual flowers, this peony is one of the most distinct and forms a really good garden plant. (M).

*Red Charm (D) (Glasscock 1944). Fantastic hybrid between *P. lactiflora* and *P. officinalis* resulting in a sturdy plant with really deep blood red flowers. They have large cup shaped guard petals and a centre of similarly coloured petaloids. A very early flowering peony, useful for stretching the season. Grows to about 90cms in height. (VE).

*Victoire de la Marne (D) (Dessert 1915). Lustrous deep double peony with medium sized blooms of deep maroon red, atop dark and stems and foliage. Later flowering. (L).

Wilbur Wright (S) (Kelway 1909). *"Very dark blackish-red; the darkest single variety. Dark stems. One medium-size flower per stem borne well above the foliage."* A singularly attractive peony, the golden stamens contrasting with the dark petals and leaves. (M).

*William F. Turner (SD) (Shaylor 1916). Deepest double red blooms of tight symmetry and form. Dark stems and foliage. This impressive peony holds a commanding position in the border. Midseason flowering. (M). **(illus p77)**

Yellow and orange

*Claire de Lune (S) (White-Wild 1954). This astonishing peony is a result of a cross between *P. lactiflora* and *P. mlokosewitschii*. The result is a peony hybrid producing single pale lemon blooms with a bright golden centre. Very early flowering usually in early May. Broad green leaves make this plant instantly recognisable even when not in flower. A singularly beautiful peony, which is quite slow growing but absolutely worth the wait. (VE). **(illus p27)**

*Coral Charm AGM (SD) (Wissing 1964). Semi double with many blooms held on strong stems. The buds open salmon pink and gradually change to orange and finally to yellow. This is a truly spectacular plant. These particular peonies thrive best in soils that are not too wet in the winter. Early flowering during May, before the traditional *P. lactiflora* types. (E). **(illus below)**

P. Coral Charm (p79)

*Coral Sunset (SD) (Wissing-Klehm 1981). Semi double blooms open a pink coral colour, then as they mature the colour changes to apricot and finally a soft yellow. With a mature plant holding flowers of all these shades simultaneously. This is one of the best of the best of all peonies. Early flowering, during May. (E). **(illus below)**

P. Coral Sunset (p79)

*Nova (S) (Saunders 1950). This is a really interesting cross between the species *P. macrophylla* and *P. mlokosewitschii*. The resulting plants have very large leaves and pale yellow flowers. Nova is one of the very first peonies to flower in the spring. Single cup shaped flowers with a multitude of yellow stamens in the centre. A really special peony for the collector, but nonetheless a really good strong growing garden plant. (VE).

*Starlight (S) (Saunders 1949). A most unusual quadruple hybrid between four different species, *P. lactiflora*, *P. macrophylla*, *P. officinalis* and *P. mlokosewitschii*. Single sulphur yellow flowers with just a hint of pink at the base of the petals. A very early peony often flowering at the beginning of May. Quite short growing to around 45cm. (VE). **(illus p86)**

Herbaceous peony breeding since 1950

Since the time of James Kelway, the energy and momentum for peony breeding has been in the USA. Professor Arthur Saunders carried much of the pioneering and key breeding work out between 1905 and 1953. James Kelway was aware of Professor Saunders's work but at the time this book was originally written, few seedlings had been bulked up enough to reach a wider audience in the UK.

Saunders, and various other enthusiasts, realized that the way ahead was to bring in other species to hybridize with *P. lactiflora*. This resulted in increasing the colour range to include true red and true yellow tones, which hitherto had been impossible. Other aims were to extend the flowering season both earlier and later in the year, and also produce plants with better foliage, that did not need staking. Some of the hybrids that have been produced are the result of complex crosses between 4 or more species. The breeding work of a few committed nurserymen continues ever onwards. But because peonies have never been successfully propagated by micro propagation techniques, it can take 20 years to get a new cultivar onto the market.

Some of the most noteworthy advances in herbaceous peony breeding are the Coral series of peonies, which introduced apricot and orange tones into the palette, particularly Coral Sunset. Buckeye Belle has amazing red flowers, and a stout habit with broad leaves. Red Charm is similar in flower to the old *P. officinalis Rubra Plena*, but the benefits of breeding and selection have produced a plant with much larger flowers with greater depth of colour, and a sturdy habit that does not need staking. The newest cultivars from the US will always be very expensive, although the cost gradually creeps down over time.

Those recent cultivars that I consider to be most garden worthy, and that are readily available from nurserymen, have been listed earlier in this chapter.

CHAPTER VI

May-flowering and specie peonies

The detailed description and care of the many other species of herbaceous peony is outside the realms of this little book. The following is a short descriptive list of some of the more readily available May-flowering herbaceous species and their hybrids. All peony species are incredibly prone to cross pollination and hybrids between two or more species are the almost the norm. It is advised to buy species peonies only from a reputable source. They are likely to be quite expensive, and it is annoying to wait two or more years for a purchase to flower, only to find that it is not as expected.

P. anomala. Bright scarlet-crimson flowers, 10cm in diameter, with golden stamens. Graceful finely cut foliage. Grows to about 45cm in height. Flowers very early in May or even in the last week of April.

P. cambessedesii **AGM**. Flowers 8cm across of a deep shade of true rosy-pink. Red filaments, yellow anthers. Purple-red carpels. Grey-green foliage with red veins and deep purple backs to the leaves and red stems. Forms a tight mounded plant rarely more than 30cm tall. This highly sought after southern European species needs full sun and really sharp drainage.

P. emodi. Beautiful large milky-white flowers. The foliage is also particularly ornamental, quite fascinatingly so in its early stage with its highly coloured bronze palmate leaves. Attains around 90cm in height. The only peony to show signs of being slightly tender.

P. Late Windflower (*P. emodi x P. veitchii*). Often sold as *P. emodi*, but the plants are of smaller stature. It is quite difficult to tell them apart. **(illus p84)**

P. Late Windflower (p83)

P. mlokosewitschii (p85)

P. **Avant Garde** *(P. lactiflora x P. wittmanniana)*. Creamy-white flushed with pink. Fine and attractive. About 90cm in height.

P. **Le Printemps** (P. *lactiflora x P. wittmanniana*). Pale biscuit-white with yellow stamens; carpels tipped crimson; medium-size flower. About 90cm in height.

P. mascula. Rosy-red with yellow anthers; the large pods with their black and coral-red seeds, are extremely effective.

P. mlokosewitschii **AGM**. This is the legendary "Molly the Witch". This gracious beauty flowers for a few days in early May, and any garden specimen is usually revered by the owner. Height around 50cm. Only purchase a plant from a source of known provenance because seed raised plants are highly variable and may have pink tinges due to cross pollination with other species. **(illus p84)**

P. officinalis **Alba Plena**. Pure white double form of the traditional cottage garden peony, growing to around 60cm in height.

P. officinalis **Anemoniflora Rosea AGM**. Carmine-rose; semi-double. Height 45cm.

P. officinalis **Anemoniflora Rubra**. Handsome deep maroon-red; semi-double. Height 45cm.

P. officinalis **Rosea Plena AGM**. Bright pure red-rose; a very pleasing colour. Double. Height 50cm.

P. officinalis **Rubra Plena AGM** ("Old Double Crimson"). The famous cottage garden peony. Large bomb shaped blooms, produced in early May. The flowers are deep crimson red, and are not scented. This peony usually benefits from staking as the blooms can be very heavy, particularly after rain. Height and spread around 50cm. **(illus p22)**

P. peregrina **Fire King;** *P. peregrina* **Otto Froebel AGM**. Rich brilliant red or lustrous rosy-scarlet. Goblet-shaped strikingly handsome flowers around 8cm across. Grows to 60-75cm in height. This unusual species and its cultivars lack the red pigment in the shoots, which emerge bright green resembling little sticks of celery. **(illus p24)**

P. tenuifolia. The "parsley leaved peony" This is one of the earliest to flower with deep scarlet to blood red blooms which are often double. Rarely grows to more than 30cm in height and spread with finely cut leaves. By early August this ephemeral little gem has receded below ground, its work for the year complete. Needs full sun and very well drained soil to thrive.

P. veitchii. Small nodding flowers in various shades of pink. Delicate fern like leaves with a bronze hue in the spring. Grows to around 50cm maximum. Early flowering in late April-early May. **(illus p25)**

P. veitchii **var.** *woodwardii*. Small nodding rose-pink flowers. Very distinct in habit and foliage. Dainty fern-like leaves, with arching stems 30-45cm high. End of May to June.

P. wittmanniana (p87)   P. Starlight (p81)

P. wittmanniana. Beautiful palest creamy-yellow with deeper golden anthers; pale green carpels with carmine tips. Red filaments. Very large bowl-shaped flowers. April to May flowering. **(illus p86)**

CHAPTER VII

Tree peonies (by Dave Root)

To those that adore them, tree peonies are the most exquisite, the most astonishing, and the most revered of all the spring flowering shrubs. No other woody plant, not even the finest magnolia can produce flowers 30cm or more in diameter from a plant just a metre or so tall. These regal blooms in a myriad of colours, not just the traditional peony pinks, reds and whites, but include orange, bronze, yellow, and darkest crimson. Some even deceive the eye, producing flashes of blue tone as light reflects off the petals. They become much loved friends in the garden. Always there, returning to flower each year. Most years a floral symphony, yet sometimes a year where a few less blooms are produced to give the plant a chance to reinvigorate itself. But always dependably and perpetually beautiful.

P. Shima-nishiki (p96)

The excitement begins in February as the buds break and the shoots for that year begins to expand. The young growths extend "pleine de vigueur", and are rich red and purple, gradually turning to green by the time blooms finish. The flower buds are soon visible, pea sized, and it is a source of wonder that these tiny spheres could possibly swell to become as large as golf balls. Peony lovers always count the blooms and watch each one develop as lovingly as a hen incubating her clutch of eggs.

A well grown plant should not need any support, but it is inevitable that the occasional stem might just need staking as the flowers open. The heavy buds and sail like flowers can put undue strain on the most woody of boughs and it is a heartbreaking moment to find an almost open bud snapped off and on the ground after a windy night.

Planting

When planting tree peonies the junction of the graft with the stock should be 5-8cm below the surface; this will encourage the graft itself to root. If you plant is pot grown from a reputable nursery it will have already been planted at the correct depth, and all that is required is to plant at the same soil level in the ground. Garden centres often stock young tree peony plants where the graft union is clearly visible. These must be planted very deeply otherwise they rarely succeed. Keep your eye on any shoots which arise from below soil level. If the leaves are the same as that of the tree peony, leave them intact for they are to be encouraged. However if the shoots are glossy like the herbaceous peony then they should be removed because they will take over and potentially kill the tree peony.

In my experience, tree peonies will thrive satisfactorily in both full sun and full shade, but the most sensational blooms always arise on the plants that are in light shade. The colours are richer and the blooms last longer. Chose a place where the air moves freely. This helps prevent the occurrence of botrytis in the developing shoots.

Tree peonies can be grown in pots for some years. Choose a pot of some 45cm in diameter, and a compost which is predominantly good garden loam. The traditional mix of John Innes No3 would be ideal, but alas, compost made to the true recipe is very difficult to find these days. Be careful not to overwater, and keep the pot itself out of the sun, because the roots hate getting too hot. A wonderful benefit of a pot grown plant is that it may be kept in an exposed and cold part of the garden during the winter, and then bought right up to a doorway or window from March onwards, so that the developing buds and flowers can be enjoyed to maximum effect.

P. Duchess of Marlborough (p94)

Pruning

Tree peonies benefit from regular pruning. This merely amounts to tidying the plant and removing any dead wood. It is sufficient to cut off the end of the flower stems above the top joint of the leaves after blooming. In early spring, cut each shoot back to the topmost live bud. Plants which have become gaunt and leggy should be pruned back to 15cm from the ground in order to induce underground buds to grow and make for a shorter more bushy plant. This somewhat drastic pruning can be carried out over two years if the gardener is of a nervous constitution! This also allows the plant to continue flowering without losing all of the flower buds for that year. An ideal sized plant is around 90-120cm in height with a profusion of stems arising from the base or below ground. Some shoots of flowering age wood, with younger juvenile shoots coming up to replace them ensures a good continuity of flowering from one year to the next.

Propagation

Tree peonies are not easy to propagate from division or layers, and nurserymen graft them on roots of *P. lactiflora*. They are at first slow to grow; plants as supplied are usually two to three years from being grafted and have woody stems 15-30cm high. But even such comparatively small plants surprise occasionally by producing in their first season a flower or two of a size out of all proportion to that of the plant.

Moving

There is no anguish necessary if a tree peony needs to be moved. Even a large plant can be dug up and moved to a new location provided it is done in the autumn once the old foliage has dropped. They are no more difficult to re-establish than any other deciduous shrub. Just respect that the flowers in the first year subsequent to relocation might be a little smaller. A good feed of general fertilizer at the time of moving, and again in the spring, will ensure that normal service is quickly resumed!

Pests and diseases

The comments for tree peonies are the same as for the herbaceous peonies (p40-41).

The best garden tree peonies

Tree peonies are still generally grouped together under the species name "suffruticosa" which is agreed by those that understand them, to be an obsolete generalisation. Most are actually complex hybrids derived from several different Chinese peony species over two thousand years. The following is a list of the most easily obtained cultivars. Most will attain a general height of 90-120cm and a spread of around 90cm. The exact size varies depending on location, age, pruning regime and cultivar. The tree peony season runs from mid-April until the end of May. Those cultivars which are particularly early or late are stated accordingly in the text.

Akashigata. Pale lavender pink with a faint magenta stripe running through the centre of each petal. Very long lasting flowers, which open slowly over several days. Broad bright green foliage, which emerges purple tinged in the spring. **(illus p93)**

Alice Palmer. Open saucer shaped flowers of mauve pink petals, edged with white. The petals incurve gracefully, particularly apparent when the flower partially closes up at night. The stems are robust and the foliage has a distinct silvery blue sheen. This marvellous tree peony takes a little time to establish and ultimately makes a stunning specimen plant.

P. Akashigata (p92)

P. Cardinal Vaughan (p94)

P. Duchess of Kent (p94)

P. Kokuryunishiki (p94)

P. Koshinoyuki (p94)

P. Mrs. William Kelway (p94)

Cardinal Vaughan. Large saucer shaped blooms of deep episcopal purple, with a sumptuous richness of colour. A most worthwhile garden shrub, which is highly recommended for a first time grower. Early flowering, so a useful plant to extend the flowering season. **(illus p93)**

Duchess of Kent. Tulip shaped buds open slowly over several days to reveal large double flowers of a clear deep rose. As the flowers mature they start to take on an unusual violet hue, which can even shimmer with a hint of blue. This is a vigorous growing plant, which flowers freely from a young age. The stems are an attractive red and the red leaf stalks give continued interest when not in flower. Later flowering. **(illus p93)**

Duchess of Marlborough. One of the finest and most famous of all the tree peonies. Large semi double saucer shaped blooms with bright flesh pink petals. This has been a firm favorite for more than 100 years. The flowers have been known to be over 30cm in diameter on a mature plant. Mid season flowering. **(illus p90)**

Kokuryunishiki. Amazing flowers, which are deep maroon purple with irregular white stripes, down the outside of the outer petals. **(illus p93)**

Koshinoyuki. Unusual green buds swell as the flower develops and look like small green cabbages. Upon opening the huge double blooms are faintly flushed ivory but soon turn to a glistening white. A splendid strong growing variety, which is remarkably free flowering, with good grey green foliage. **(illus p93)**

Mrs. William Kelway. Huge dinner plate sized blooms of the purest milky white, without any hint of pink. The flowers are semi-double, in some years more so and in other years less so. Bright golden stamens peer out from between the petals. **(illus p93)**

Nigata Akashigata. Pale blush pink flowers with a deep magenta stripe through the centre of each petal. The very spectacular blooms open while still small and develop in size and colour over several days before displaying their 'fully open' characteristics. The flowers are remarkably robust. Very distinct foliage. **(illus p98)**

P. Renkaku (p95)

Renkaku. Pure white dinner plate sized, semi double blooms with golden centres. The flowers open from pointed buds, and the petals are delicately fimbriated at the edges. This is a really beautiful tree peony and one of the earliest to flower. **(illus above)**

Rinpo. A most magnificent tree peony of ancient origin. The large semi double blooms open very flat. The colour is described by the Japanese as Botan purple and the petals have silvery edges. A very late flowering plant. The buds tantalise for what seems like weeks before they finally fully open.

Shima-nishiki. Fabulous and unique tree peony with irregularly variegated flowers, some red and white, others white and red. Each flower an individual. **(illus p88)**

Shimane Hakugan. Elegant blooms of pure milk white. In the centre of each flower a ring of golden stamens surrounds a single rich red carpel. It is outstandingly beautiful in its simplicity. **(illus below)**

P. Shimane Hakugan (p96)

Shimane Seidai. Bright rose pink blooms that are semi double when the plant is young, but become progressively more double and substantial as the plant grows older. A robust growing shrub, which will flower reliably every year. **(illus below)**

Shimano-fuji. Immense open cup shaped blooms of a rich shade of lavender pink with darker flares at the base of the petals. Bright grey green foliage. Late flowering, a good choice to extend the season. **(illus below)**

P. Shimane Seidai (p97)   *P. Shimano-fuji (p97)*

Tamafuyo. Blowsy semi double blooms of pale apple blossom pink. The flowers have a distinct sweet scent. Tree peonies overall are not particularly scented, so this is a real treat. The foliage has a purple tint until quite late in the spring providing a beautiful foil to the flowers. **(illus front cover, p113)**

Yachiyo Tsubaki. One of the best of all tree peonies and ideal for a first foray into these beautiful plants. Large semi double flowers of bright coral pink with silky smooth petals. The foliage is a distinct smokey bronze and a perfect foil to the flowers. Vigorous and dependable, quickly forming an attractive garden shrub with year round interest. Even the winter stems are an attractive pinky red. **(illus p98)**

P. Nigata Akashigata (p95)

P. Yachiyo Tsubaki (p97)

Hybrid yellow varieties (*Paeonia x lemoinei*)

Chromatella. Very clear sulphur-yellow. In other respects similar to Souvenir de Maxime Cornu.

L'Esperance. Single flowers of pale amber yellow to richer shades, and spotted carmine at the base. The edges of the petals are tinged pink. This cultivar is incredibly rare nowadays, probably due to an inherent lack of vigour within the plant. Anyone owning one should cherish and guard it.

Madame Louis Henri. Cup-shaped single flowers, about 15cm in breadth with waved petals of bright deep carmine, buff and pink, shaded salmon and coppery yellow, with purple markings at the base of the petals and orange-yellow stamens. Very sweetly scented.

Souvenir de Maxime Cornu. Every stem carries one to three very large full double flowers, 15-18cm in diameter, of perfect form, with petals of a brilliant yellow, heavily shaded orange-salmon. The colour intensifies over several days as the bloom matures. Very fragrant and lasting. The hanging flowers are a natural trait of this spectacular peony, and it should be celebrated rather than dismissed. If planted at the top of a flight of steps, the flowers can be admired from underneath. **(illus p100)**

American hybrid cultivars

Black Pirate AGM. This is one of the aristocrats of tree peonies. Notoriously difficult to propagate but no more difficult to grow than any other tree peony. Dramatic, deep mahogany red, semi-double flowers, which open at an angle like small trumpets. Plentiful blooms and finely dissected foliage that continues to be attractive throughout the growing season. Once established this hybrid will grow vigorously forming a shrub of great garden merit. One of the last plants to flower in May. **(illus p100)**

P. Souvenir de Maxime Cornu (p99)

P. Black Pirate (p99)

Chinese Dragon. Wonderful and sought after tree peony which has the merit of being one of the first to flower in the spring. Single flowers of the violet maroon which shimmer with a blue tint as they catch the light. This needs to be seen to be believed! Highly dissected purple foliage is retained till early summer before turning to green. **(illus p102)**

Golden Isle. A superlative hybrid of *P. lutea*, bred in America. Semi double to fully double bright yellow flowers with red flares at the base of the petals. Forms a vigorous shrub with bright fresh green foliage. Late flowering. Unlike many of the yellow tree peonies this cultivar does not hang its flowers, and the large yellow blooms stand proud for all to see! **(illus p103)**

P. High Noon (p101)

High Noon AGM. This is without a doubt the easiest to grow and most rewarding of all the hybrid tree peonies. Medium sized semi-double yellow flowers with raspberry flares at the base of each petal. The blooms have a strong fragrance, which is quite unusual for tree peonies as a whole. Forms a vigorous shrub with dissected foliage and can soon attain 1.5m in height. An added bonus is that it may often throw up a few extra flowers in the autumn. **(illus p101)**

Renown. Delectable blooms of a unique copper strawberry colour. Semi double medium size flowers borne in profusion. The foliage is quite dissected with attractive red edges to the leaves in spring. **(illus p103)**

Vesuvian. The very last tree peony to flower. It is closely related to Black Pirate but the flowers are double and a little smaller. This is a little gem and ideal for overlapping the tree peonies with the herbaceous peonies. Easily grown but difficult to propagate, which means that it will always be a little more expensive.

P. Chinese Dragon (p101)

P. Golden Isle (p101)   P. Renown (p102)

Chinese tree peonies

Tree peonies have been grown in China for over two thousand years. They were grown in the royal palaces of the emperors, and were revered for their beauty. Some were deemed so special that only the Emperor himself was allowed to set eyes on them, and anyone else daring to take a look would be executed!

In recent years there has been a flood of cheap tree peonies with exotic sounding Chinese names onto the market. Whilst these plants potentially represent good value for money, there are also pitfalls to their purchase and cultivation. The plants are usually severely root pruned for export and establishment is slow and not always successful. Chinese winters and summers are much colder and hotter than those we usually experience, and this can reduce the flowering potential of these plants; the lack of a frozen winter will often mean that the plant does not go into full dormancy, and the subsequent shoot growth and flower production can be poor. Cultivar names are often muddled, and there is a good chance that the name on the label may not be the actual plant purchased. Having said all of this, there are some wonderful Chinese cultivars in colours and shades not seen even in the Japanese tree peonies, including greens and bi coloured pinks and whites.

Species tree peonies

P. delavayi. Small single flowers around 5cm in diameter. Most usually crimson red, but hybridization with *P. ludlowii* readily occurs producing individuals with orange, striped, or even yellow flowers. Dissected foliage is attractive. Forms a bushy shrub up to 1.5m high and broad. **(illus below)**

P. ludlowii (formerly P. lutea). Small single yellow flowers around 5cm in diameter. Usually buttercup yellow, but occasional plants with orange striped flowers may arise. Huge bright green dissected leaves. Specimens may attain 3m in height and spread. Regular pruning is usually the best way to keep this peony under control. **(illus below)**

P. delavayi (p104)   P. ludlowii (p104)

P. ostii. Spectacular species which is naturally quite variable. Large single flower up to 15cm in diameter that may be pure white, blush pink, through to mid pink. Can ultimately attain 1.5m in height. **(illus p105)**

P. potaninii. Low growing shrub usually less than 1m in height but spreading by underground runners. Flowers usually yellow or white, but darker forms may be occasionally produced. Attractive dissected foliage. **(illus below)**

P. ostii (p104)   *P. potaninii (p105)*

P. rockii & *P.* Joseph Rock

Paeonia rockii is arguably the most spectacular of all garden shrubs. It will grow to 2m in height and once established it will be the star of the spring garden, flowering in early may with large purest white blooms with a deep purple blotch at the centre of each petal. The flowers are sweetly scented and the foliage is delicate, with rich autumn colour. **(illus p106)**

One of the most sought after of all plants, *P. rockii* originates from China where it was grown in monasteries and revered and worshipped by the monks who lived there. It first came to Europe as seed from a single specimen seen by Joseph Rock in the Choni Monastery in Gansu Province in 1926. Muslim soldiers subsequently destroyed the monastery in 1928. A few specimens were grown from this seed; however all were slightly variable from each other. Up until the turn of 21st century, anybody wanting a plant had to pay dearly for a specimen grafted from one of these seedlings.

P. rockii (p105)

However in the past 10 years "*P. rockii*" has been exported in thousands by Chinese nurserymen. There are hundreds of named cultivars all of the style of the plant found by Joseph Rock, although many are inferior with poor and pale blotches. The colour can range from white, creamy yellow, pink, red and purple. Many of these are astoundingly beautiful in their own right, and overwhelmingly scented.

But if your desire is for the iconic black and white flower, it is essential to view the specimen you want to buy in flower before you part with your money, to ensure that you know precisely what you are paying for.

Intersectional hybrids

These are the future of peonies. James Kelway may have been aware when the first cross between a tree peony and a herbaceous peony was successfully made in 1948 in Japan, although the first flowers were not seen until 1964. It is possible that James Kelway may have attempted this difficult hybridization experiment himself. 60 years of refining and experimentation have begun to produce plants that exhibit all the best characteristics of their contrasting parents. Intersectional peonies produce short stubby stems usually no more than 10cm high that superficially resemble tree peonies.

The foliage is usually exceptionally broad and lush, forming rounded bushes up to 90cm x 90cm, although some are smaller. Flowers are usually semi double or single around 10cm in diameter. The range of colours is astonishing. The early hybrids were all yellow, but more recent hybrids are white, copper, orange, lavender, deep red, and pink. They are vigorous in habit and tend be later flowering, after the tree peonies and around the same time as the lactifloras.

The slow method of propagation by division means that these wondrous plants are still quite expensive although they are gradually reducing in price, particularly the oldest hybrids such as Bartzella and Yellow Crown, which are now no more expensive than the best lactifloras.

The following is a short list of a few of the most noteworthy and available hybrids.

P. Callie's Memory (p109)   *P. Canary Brilliant ((p109)*

P. First Arrival (p109)

Bartzella AGM. This beautiful yellow peony is perhaps the most popular of all. Intense sulphur yellow double flowers and deep green broad foliage. It makes a vigorous bush up to about 75cm in height. Late flowering, it is a joy to behold.

Callie's Memory. Exceptional peony. Semi double or double flowers with creamy buff petals and orange red flares. Bushy leafy plants which look healthy and glossy right up to the autumn frosts. Height 75cms. **(illus p108)**

Canary Brilliant. Semi double apricot blooms with red tinged edges fading to deep yellow with red flares. Absolutely sensational in full bloom. Very vigorous, with deeply cut dark green leaves. Height 75cms. **(illus p108)**

First Arrival. Very large flowers, which can range in colour from lavender pink to a quite deep magenta pink, the colour varying from year to year. A free flowering plant with dark green foliage providing a deep foil for the amazing flowers. Forms beautiful bushes up to 75cm high. **(illus p108)**

Hillary. Semi-double exquisite blooms of apricot orange. The petals have a light magenta overlay and deep red flares at the base. Dark green foliage forms a vigorous bush with a height and spread of around 75cm.

Julia Rose. Magical flowers which open from a red bud, soon changing to tones of orange with purple flushed edges. Dark green foliage. Height and spread approximately 75cm.

Kopper Kettle. Semi-double blooms of a blend of apricot with some purple flushing to some of the petals, and even some purple and yellow flecking. A vigorous growing plant with a rich spicy fragrance. Height around 75cm.

Morning Lilac. Extraordinary blooms of deep lilac, which slowly pale in strong sunlight. A highly rewarding plant, which can carry dozens of blooms on a mature specimen. Height around 80cm.

Pastel Splendour. Crimson edged yellow petals and red flares. The single flowers are strongly scented. Wonderful and highly sought after. Height around 75cm. **(illus p110)**

Scarlet Heaven. Single flowered variety with bright bold scarlet blooms. Since most true scarlet peonies are early spring flowering, this one really extends the colour range of late flowering peonies. Deep dark foliage.

Sonoma Kaleidoscope. Recent Japanese introduction. The flowers are single and orange-yellow with some wine markings towards the centre of the flower.

Yellow Crown. One of the original hybrids and yet still one of the most charming, with large semi-double bright yellow flowers. A really good garden plant with bright green foliage forming a nicely rounded bush of 75cm height and spread. **(illus below)**

P. Pastel Splendour (p109)

P. Yellow Crown (p110)

CHAPTER VIII

A brief historical sketch of Paeonia

The mists of antiquity in North-East Asia do not hide the fact that the people of China appreciated the startling beauty of the peony even in remote ages. From the earliest period of which we have knowledge and probably from still earlier times at which we can only guess, Chinese artists used the peony in flower and foliage for their drawings on porcelain and embroideries on silk, as Japanese artists later did for their colour prints. These beautiful and accurate designs are mainly of the Moutan or "Tree" peony, plants of which first reached Europe as far as is known, in 1789, followed by the next introduction in 1887, and less frequently of the herbaceous species *P. lactiflora* which had arrived in Europe as far back as 1548.

P. Kelway's Brilliant (p66)

The following account written as early as 1850, of tree peonies in China, is of interest:

"I walked onwards to the Moutan Nurseries. They are situated near the village of Fa-Who, about five or six miles west of Shanghae, and in the midst of an extensive cotton country. On the road I met a number of coolies, each carrying two baskets filled with Moutans in full flower, which were on their way to the markets for sale. When I reached the gardens, I found many of the plants in full bloom, and certainly extremely handsome. The purple and lilac-coloured kinds were particularly striking. In the gardens of the Mandarins it is not unusual to meet with a tree peony of great size. There was one plant near Shanghae which produced between three and four hundred blooms every year." (*The Gardener's Chronicle, December 28th, 1850.*)

The peony is still, as it has always been, one of the chief glories of China. This feeling is evident in the following verse from a modern Chinese song:

"There is a gruesome storm in the Garden of the Peonies,
And the raindrops are like stones, and the wind like a broom.
Yet though the petals fall like lovers' tears,
The flowers will blossom to the end of time."

(The "Garden"= China; 'storm"= the Japanese Invasion.)

In modern times peonies bid fair to be the most popular of all hardy plants, owing not only to their beauty and usefulness as a cut flower, but also to their proving hardier than the rose, rhododendron or azalea, and to their flourishing in both acid and alkaline soils.

Notable peonies other than *P. suffruticosa* and *P. lactiflora*, with the dates of their first discovery by Europeans, are *P. delavayi* (1884, Western China); *P. lutea*, (1883, Western China); *P. veitchii* var. *woodwardii,* (Kansu); *P.*

emodi, which pushed itself, probably many centuries ago, as far as the Himalaya range of mountains, where it was found by a European as late as 1868; *P. brownii*, reported from North America in 1826, this is interesting as it may have come there with, or at any rate by the same route as the South and North American "Indians" from their original home in Mongolia; *P. wittmanniana* (1842, Eastern Caucasus); *P. mlokosewitschii* (1900, Northern Persia); *P. obovata* (1859, Siberia); *P. anomala* (1877, Central Asia); *P. officinalis* (1548, Southern Europe); *P. tenuifolia* (1765, Crimea and Transylvania); *P. mascula* (Europe and Levant); *P. peregrina* (1583 and 1629, Balkans); *P. arietina* (Greece, Levant); *P. cambessedesii* (1896, Majorca and Corsica); *P. veitchii* (1907, China). There are records of many other species and sub-species but the foregoing are among those of most interest for our gardens.

P. Tamafuyo (p97)

One reads that the word *"Paeonia"* traces back to its mention by an ancient writer, Theophrastus, "a friend of Aristotle and Plato", who died 285 BC. It is said to commemorate a physician named Paeon, who used its roots in medicine. Our great-grandmothers who spoke of the piny-rose were near to the accepted pronunciation of the Latin form.

We may safely say that the honour of raising artificially or by accident the first variety whether from *P. suffruticosa* or *P. lactiflora*, would belong to a Chinaman. But those varieties were not allowed to be exported at that time, except possibly to Japan.

In Europe, French nurserymen commenced the raising of varieties before the middle of the nineteenth century. Of the herbaceous species *P. lactiflora*, a certain Monsieur Lemoine raised a freak which he called *P. prolifera tricolor*, in 1825. M.Donkelaer raised Festiva, in 1838; M.Delache, Rubra Triumphant, in 1840; and a goodly number of seedlings were named and distributed from that time onwards by Guerin (1845), Crousse (1845), Calot, Verdier, Gombault, Miellez, followed by Méchin, Dessert, Lemoine, Doriat and others. The honour was reserved for my grandfather James Kelway and his son William to be the first English raisers of new varieties. They were pioneers in popularising the peony in Great Britain; and also in introducing it on a large scale from 1890 onwards, to North America. Their work with peonies dates from about the year 1865, and it has been continued for sixty years by the present writer, of the third generation of the family.

CHAPTER IX

The Peony Valley (by Dave Root)

Of all the achievements of the Kelway family, Peony Valley is one of their most famous. This corner of Barrymore Farm had always been James Kelway's trial ground for his new peony seedlings. It is a 6-acre field through which a rivulet flows, once serving the Mill that sat in its centre and of which the foundations still remain.

Peony Valley in 1929

The picture above shows a view of the Valley in 1929. The archway marks the entrance to the Valley, and still exists. It has been recently restored and was used as the centrepiece of Kelways' centenary Chelsea Flower Show exhibit in 2013.

Row upon row of plants were grown and flowered, to be scrupulously inspected by James and judged on the floral merit and also on the habit of the plant, the foliage and the general garden worthiness of each. Only the best would pass his repeated inspection over several years and be introduced in the latest "Manual of Horticulture" as a new variety. The best of the best would be named after noteworthy individuals and personalities of the era such as Lord Kitchener and Sir Edward Elgar, whilst the most supreme seedlings of all would be named after the members of his own family, such as Beatrice Kelway and Boy Kelway, or would have the prestigious "Kelway's" prefix such as Kelway's Glorious or Kelway's Malmaison.

James Kelway inspecting peonies in Peony Valley in 1935

The London to Penzance railway line has always run along the southern boundary of the nursery and it is long reputed that during the time that the peonies were in flower, the trains would slow down so that the passengers could admire the peonies. It is even suggested that in some years a temporary railway station called "Peony Valley Halt" was erected so that the passengers could alight and wander through the flowers.

Peony Valley in 2012

At the time of writing (December 2012) there are plans to plant a new peony collection still within the original area, but closer to the car park of the garden centre where the peonies can be more easily seen, and also where fewer plants of more cultivars can be arranged in a smaller area to make viewing and the comparison between cultivars, easier, and also make maintenance more practical.

In 1929, Marion Cran, who was the first woman to regularly broadcast about gardening on the British Broadcasting Corporation, visited Kelways and made the following broadcast.

> *"Have you ever walked in the Valley of Peonies and watched the different shades of blooms in the sun? There is such a valley in the West Country where the sun shines down on millions of glorious peonies.*
> *As you go down the hill road to the valley, the fragrance comes floating up to you, borne on the wind. Very sweet and fresh and keen. When once you have been there you come out different; you have been in an enchanted place and you are restless and unsatisfied until you can grow some of those beautiful flowers for yourself, to make a new memory of that day when you first saw the valley."*

CHAPTER X

Last word

To what does all that I have written here amount? May I sum it up in a philosophy of the peony? In the first place, that whilst there are multitudes of beautiful flowers and plants in a world of interesting flowers, the peony in its present-day types is certainly in the first rank, but that it has been in this country markedly overlooked and somewhat neglected.

One reason I have already referred to: people are acquainted with the cottage favourite, the Old Double Crimson, and they suspect that other peonies of which they have no knowledge would be equally commonplace. I have written in vain if this idea has not been dispelled from the minds of my readers. The Old Double Crimson certainly affords a brilliant bit of colour earlier in the year but occupies a niche of its own.

Another cause for their lack of universal popularity is that supplying peony plants has not been a proposition attractive to nurserymen. Like many things of solid worth peonies take some time to build themselves up and it has paid nurserymen better to propagate and recommend flowers that take less time to grow into plants fit to send out. In fact professional growers in general have taken "a short view" and have put the labour of their hands and the value of their land to a quicker turnover. This, and the fact that plants that are simply divisions from stools take two or three years before producing fine flowers, has rather unfairly given peonies generally the reputation of needing several years before they flower.

It is true that the nurseryman who is a peony specialist has to allow two to three years for his young plants to become large enough for him to distribute, but such plants in an amateur's garden will produce a blossom or two the same June and will flower well the following season. From thence onwards flowers will be borne in increasing abundance for an indefinite period, and with very little attention, as it is not a plant that has to be thinned out or divided and transplanted every few years.

There is the point of comparative value. With the honourable exception of books, what equivalent value is to be secured today? What equivalent pleasure, permanent or recurring?

My conclusion must be that in the peony one has consummate loveliness and a perennial joy in return for a minimum of expenditure in money and labour.

P. Joy of Life (p55)

Acknowledgments

Thank you to Clodagh Barker (née Kelway) and the Kelway family for giving me permission to revise your grandfather's book. Thanks to Janet Seaton, Kelways Official Historian, for your help and guidance throughout this project. Thank you Pete Fairburn for the cover design, and Andrew Lee for handling the publishing.

My gratitude to the late James Kelway for writing the first edition, and inspiring the second; I hope you approve of our joint effort.

To my darling wife Sonya, and my very tall son Tristan, thank you for putting up with yet another reason for me to fail you. I love you both.

Picture credits

All pictures copyright Dave Root and Kelways Plants Ltd. Except Dave Root (back cover) Pete Fairburn, and James Kelway (back cover) Clodagh Barker.

INDEX OF PEONIES